Let's Get Ready for First Grade

Literacy Centers, Strategies, and Assessments

Laura Townsend

Illustrated by Robert Masheris

Rigby Best Teachers Press

An imprint of Rigby

Dedication:
To Brad, who keeps the kid in me alive.
Thanks for all your love and support!

For more information about other books from Rigby Best Teachers Press, please contact
Rigby at 1-800-822-8661 or visit **www.rigby.com**

Editor: Mary Susnis
Executive Editor: Georgine Cooper
Designer: Bob Masheris
Design Production Manager: Tom Sjoerdsma
Cover Illustrator: Bob Masheris
Cover Photographer: Sharon Hoogstraten
Interior Illustrator: Bob Masheris

07 06 05 04 03
10 9 8 7 6 5 4 3 2 1

Printed in the United States of America.

ISBN: 0-7398-7596-5
Let's Get Ready for First Grade: Literacy Centers, Strategies, and Assessments

Table of Contents

Introduction

Many of us remember the excitement and the butterflies in our stomachs on the first day of kindergarten. Off we went to school with our backpacks full school supplies. We couldn't wait to get to school where we would surely learn to read and write, just like the older children did.

Kindergarten is the foundation on which a child's formal education is built. Kindergarten teachers have a tremendous duty to fulfill–to begin children's education in reading and writing and to instill in children a love of learning. Kindergarten teachers have the job of lighting the fire within and creating an environment that will foster positive feelings toward all their educational experiences to come.

With the help of this book, you can structure your kindergarten class so children begin their formal education in a positive and literacy-rich environment. By providing children with learning opportunities that are balanced and engaging, you will help your children prepare for first grade.

This book provides you with the building blocks needed to create a balanced literacy environment in your kindergarten classroom. On the pages that follow, you will find resource lists of books to share with children, tools for authentic assessment, ideas for literacy centers that will engage children, and tips for making connections with parents. With the help of this book, your kindergarten curriculum will come alive with possibilities!

Conditions of Learning

Brian Cambourne (1988) tells us that children need to be engaged in order to learn. After watching children in the classroom, he discovered that classrooms with engaged learners had several of the same conditions present. These conditions of learning include:

- Immersion
- Demonstration
- Expectation
- Response
- Responsibility
- Use
- Approximation

As you plan activities for children, keep these conditions in mind.

Immersion

Children need to be immersed in language, both oral and written. When they are immersed in language, they will learn the rules and conventions of language more naturally. You can immerse children in language by providing lots of opportunities for meaningful talk in your classroom. As children come into the classroom, greet them with a hello and ask them a question specific to them. Vary the questions you ask each child daily to elicit different responses. Encourage children to share stories about the events in their lives. Find time to carry on meaningful conversations with individuals and small groups of children.

In addition to oral conversations, surround children with printed language. Immerse children in print by providing them with lots of books to peruse. Put songs and rhymes on charts which children can revisit on their own or with a friend. Label classroom objects. Write down children's experiences for them. Provide them with daily opportunities to hear and see language.

Expectation

Set expectations for children and help them to understand these expectations. Treat children in a way that shows you expect them to learn. After all, what parent does not expect his or her child to learn to talk, learn to read, and learn to write? By providing children with opportunities to practice their developing skills, you are setting expectations for them.

Also encourage children to set expectations for themselves. Ask them what they want to learn while they are in kindergarten. As the year goes along, include them in decision-making by asking them what they want to learn when they are at school.

Literacy centers provide opportunities for learning expectations to be set. After explaining each center, you should expect children to be responsible learners as they are involved in these centers.

Responsibility

Teachers can provide many opportunities for children to learn, but it is the child's responsibility to make the most of those opportunities. Children are responsible for learning from daily experiences and applying new knowledge to future situations. For instance, when you show children how to write their names, they may only attend to the beginning letter at first. For a time, they may practice the uppercase letter and scribble the rest of the name. However, as you continue to model, eventually children will take the responsibility to learn another letter or two. Before long, children will be writing their whole name without any help. This development occurs because the child has taken responsibility for learning.

In a balanced literacy classroom, teachers gradually release responsibility to children. As you look at the components in a balanced literacy classroom, modeled reading (Read Alouds) and modeled writing leave most of the learning responsibility on the teacher's shoulders. As children become more involved in shared reading and shared writing experiences, they share the learning responsibility with the teacher. In guided reading and guided writing situations, children continue to increase the amount of responsibility they take on. And finally, in independent reading and independent writing, the full learning responsibility lies on children's shoulders.

Approximation

A baby might say "D...d...d..." for "Daddy". That's approximation! Parents instinctively know what a little one wants when he or she points to Daddy and says, "D...d...d...." Encouraging approximations in your kindergarten classroom is extremely important in children's literacy development. As children learn new skills and strategies, it is important to provide a risk-free environment in which they can try out these new skills and strategies. By encouraging approximation, you are providing this kind of environment. Our first attempts at learning something new are often flawed, but we learn from those approximations, each time improving upon our skills. For example, when a child reads his or her story to you, the word *cat* may be the only correctly spelled word. Praising the approximations such as *pla* for *play* encourages the child to continue work on his or her spelling development.

Approximations lead to wonderful learning opportunities for children and wonderful assessment opportunities for teachers. Encourage children in your classroom to approximate and enjoy watching their developmental growth as they do.

Demonstration

Demonstration (modeling by you, the proficient reader and writer) should happen on a daily basis. Many of us learn best when we can watch someone do what we are learning to do. For example, when learning to play golf, it is helpful to watch a proficient golfer swing the club and hear the golfer explain each step in the process.

It is so important for children to see teachers and other adults reading and writing every day. They need to watch a proficient learner work his or her way through the task at hand. As you demonstrate for children, explain your thought processes along the way. Children can learn a great deal more when you share your thoughts with them.

When children work in small groups, they also demonstrate strategies and skills for each other. Encourage children to share their thought processes when they are involved in shared and guided reading and writing experiences. For example, during a shared writing experience, the class may be working out the spelling of the word *school*. Ask volunteers to share how they know what letter comes at the end of the word. By encouraging children to demonstrate their knowledge, you are allowing them to be engaged learners.

Use

Practice makes perfect sums up the necessity for children to use what they are learning. When possible, provide opportunities that allow children to use what they are learning in context rather than in isolation. For example, if children are learning to read and write the high-frequency word *the*, include many opportunities for children to read the word in the context of sentences and stories and to write the word in the context of a sentence. After children have had opportunities to see and use the word *the* in context, they can further practice this new learning in a variety of contexts including making the word with magnetic letters, writing the word in sand or shaving cream, and finding the word in other texts. By working in a whole-to-part sequence, children will more likely understand the new skill and use it as they work independently. Give children daily opportunities to use what they know and are learning.

Response

Respond to children's efforts. As educators and self-esteem boosters, it is so important to give children feedback. Tell them what they did right. Let them know that you have noticed their improvements. Answering a child's question is a type of response, too. A child knows if he or she got the message across to you by the way you answer.

When you set up your daily schedule, it is important to build in time for children to share and for their classmates to respond. Each day, build in five minutes at the end of your center time for children to share the activities in which they were involved. This time allows children to respond to their peers. For example, if John has drawn a picture that he wants to share with the class, allow his classmates to give him feedback. If several children read a Big Book, they may want to respond to each other's thoughts about the story–*I liked that part of the story, too. It was so funny.* This sharing time allows you to encourage children to further their learning.

What to Look For at the Beginning of Kindergarten

At the start of the year, assess children's basic reading and writing knowledge to help inform your early instruction. As you look at the strengths and weaknesses of each child, you will want to look for the following things:

- Can the child listen to stories read aloud without frequently interrupting the reader?

- Can the child pay attention for a short time period?

- Can the child follow simple two- and three-step directions?

- Can the child talk in complete sentences of at least five to six words in length?

- Can the child tell a story about pictures?

- Can the child identify his or her name?

- Can the child write his or her name? (Letters may be capital, lowercase, or a mix.)

- Can the child identify **some** letters of the alphabet?

- Can the child recognize **some** environmental print or high-frequency words?

- Can the child identify **some** beginning sounds?

- Can the child identify **some** rhyming sounds?

As you assess children, you may need to spend time with small groups or individuals to help them overcome areas of difficulty. The following pages will provide some activities that can be used to help children with the basics of reading and writing.

Can the child listen to stories read aloud without frequently interrupting?

- Work with two or three children at a time. Before reading a very short story, tell the children that if they want to say something about the story, they can put their thumbs up. You will call on them to share at an appropriate pause in the story. If children wait to be called upon to share, give them some type of positive reinforcement (verbal or tactile).

- Place children who interrupt most frequently right by your side. Work out a signal such as placing a gentle hand on their shoulders to use if they interrupt at inappropriate times. This can remind them to hold their thoughts for another time.

Can the child pay attention for a designated time period?

- Place those children who have difficulty attending for a lengthy period of time right by your side. Create a non-threatening signal (a tap on the shoulder, a quick call of their name, snapping the fingers) to use as a reminder to focus on the task at hand. Children should be looking and listening for their signal.

- Creating a reward system for children who have difficulty paying attention can be highly motivating. If the child is paying attention for a designated length of time, he or she may get a token or a point. If children earn a designated number of points or tokens within an hour, they receive a certificate, a sticker, or some other reward.

Can the child follow simple two-and three-step directions?

- Working with small groups of children or one-on-one, give children two- or three-step directions. If needed, repeat the directions so they can be successful. Start with directions that require children to respond orally or physically. For example, *Stand up and touch your head* or *Turn to a friend and say your name.* Then move into directions that ask children to create something. *Draw a yellow sun and a purple flower.*

- Another fun way to help children attend to simple directions is to play *Simon Says*. Begin with simple one-step directions and gradually increase the number of directions. Once again, play this game with a small group of children. This will help children stay focused on you, the direction-giver.

Can the child talk in complete sentences of at least five to six words in length?

- As children come into the classroom, ask them a daily question. Try to ask questions that will elicit more than a one or two word answer. If the child gives you a short answer, be sure to repeat child's answer in complete sentences.

- Model for children how to speak in complete sentences. Role-playing is a great way to model this. Invite a child to ask you a question. Then respond to that child with a complete sentence. Explicitly point out to children how you responded.

Can the child tell a story about pictures?

- For children who seem to have difficulty telling a story by using the pictures, spend time working with wordless books. Wordless books require readers to make up story lines to go with the pictures. Model frequently how you tell a story using the pictures in these types of books. Then invite volunteers to add to your story.

- Draw a picture on a piece of paper. Model a story that you might tell about that picture. Then ask volunteers to tell their versions of the story. This activity can be done quickly on a daily basis with the whole class or with small groups of children. You might draw your pictures ahead of time and then spend a few minutes telling stories about your pictures. Encourage children to carry this skill over to their own pictures.

Can the child identify and write his or her name?

- It is important that a child recognize his or her name in the early days of kindergarten. For those children who do not recognize their names, model writing their names frequently. Point out where their names appear around the room. Play this name game. Spread name cards out in front of the child and read each name aloud. Ask the child to find his or her name. Challenge the child by adding more name cards.

- Continue modeling how to form the letters in the child's name and have him or her trace the letters with a finger. Then, provide the child with a name card that clearly shows his or her name. Provide a shirt box lid full of sand or shaving cream. Encourage the child to practice writing his or her name in the sand or shaving cream. You might also create sandpaper letters for the child to create a rubbing of his or her name.

Can the child identify some letters of the alphabet?

- It is not necessary for children to begin the school year knowing all of the letters of the alphabet; however, it is helpful if children are able to recognize some letters. For children who seem to lack alphabet knowledge, read a variety of alphabet books to them. After each reading, revisit the book, pointing to and identifying the letters of the alphabet.

- Working with a small group of children, play a matching game of *Go Fish* using index cards that have the letters of the alphabet on them. This will encourage children to identify the letters as they ask their peers for cards that match the cards in their hands.

Can the child recognize some environmental print or high-frequency words?

- To encourage children's recognition of environmental print start a *word wall*. Cut out examples of environmental print from newspaper ads, food packages, and fast food bags, and hang these up on the word wall. Each day read the word wall with children. Invite them to add words they know how to read.

- As you engage children in shared reading activities, point out examples of high-frequency words. One day you might focus on finding *the* in the text. Another day focus on *can* or *see*. Model writing these words in a sentence. Put the word on a word card. These cards can also be added to the word wall. Again, be sure to spend time daily reading the word wall with children.

Can the child identify some beginning sounds?

- Use children's first names to focus on beginning sounds. Play the game *I'm Going on a Picnic* encouraging children to think of something to bring on the picnic that starts with the same sound as their first name.

- Read a variety of alphabet books. As you read through the books emphasize the beginning sounds for each letter. Create your own class alphabet book. Children can cut out magazine pictures to glue onto each appropriate page. Revisit this book often with small groups where you can focus on difficult sounds.

Can the child identify some rhyming sounds?

- Read lots of nursery rhymes! Often children come to school with little exposure to nursery rhymes and their playful language. As you read and recite nursery rhymes with children, they will begin to pick up on rhyming patterns. As children become more familiar with nursery rhymes, allow them to complete the phrases. Then ask how they knew what went there, focusing on the rhyme.

- Play a rhyming word game each day. Say, *I am thinking of a word that rhymes with cat. It's like a mouse. It's called a _____.* Point out the rhyming pairs of words to children. *Yes, cat and rat rhyme.* As children become comfortable with this game, encourage volunteers to think of examples.

What to Look For at the End of Kindergarten

Children develop at different rates. Not every child learns to walk and talk at the exact same age. The same holds true for children's rates of development in reading and writing. However, there are some milestones that you want children to strive for as they end the kindergarten year and prepare to enter first grade.

As you did at the beginning of the year, you will want to take some time to observe and reflect upon the strengths and weaknesses of the children in your class. For all children, you will want to encourage the continuation of reading and writing activities at home. In some cases, you might recommend expanding the child's experiential background during the summer with family outings, park district activities, or summer programs. Summer school is also an option to consider in order to keep a child's development progressing.

In the Parent-Teacher Connections beginning on page 132, you will find activities that you can share with parents. These activities will give parents the tools they need to help their children at home throughout the school year or over the summer months.

Milestones for Children as They Leave Kindergarten

- Can the child pay attention for a short time period?

- Can the child follow simple three- to four-step directions?

- Can the child respond with an appropriate and grammatically correct response to most questions asked of him or her?

- Can the child retell a story?

- Can the child write his or her name using an initial capital letter followed by lowercase letters?

- Can the child identify a *majority* of the letters of the alphabet?

- Can the child recognize environmental print or high-frequency words? (See Appendix C on page 156 for a list of the top twenty-five most common words.) Can the child can read these words.?

- Can the child identify a *majority* of initial consonant sounds?

- Can the child identify rhyming sounds on a consistent basis? Consider if the child can make rhyming words using common rime patterns such as *ill*, *at*, and so on.

- Does the child understand a *majority* of the concepts about print? (See page 96 for a Concepts About Print checklist.)

- Does the child exhibit many of the emergent reading and writing behaviors? (See pages 97-98 for reading checklists. See pages 125-126 for writing checklists.)

Balanced Literacy: What is it?

Balanced literacy is a teaching approach that has at its core the following components:

- Modeled Reading/Read Alouds
- Shared Reading
- Guided Reading
- Independent Reading

- Modeled Writing
- Shared Writing
- Guided Writing
- Independent Writing

Beyond these components, balanced literacy is so much more. Many veteran teachers have seen the educational pendulum swing from one loosely organized system to another highly structured, program-driven end. Balanced literacy seems to fall between these two extremes. This teaching approach provides several benefits to children.

Benefits of Balanced Literacy

- Children are immersed in high-quality literature on a daily basis.

- Children are provided with direct instruction on a daily basis.

- Age-appropriate activities are planned.

- Children's strengths and weaknesses are identified. This information is used to plan activities.

- A variety of learning styles are addressed in each day's activities.

- Children are grouped in a variety of flexible ways–sometimes by ability, other times by interest.

- Children begin at their developmental level, and the teacher moves them forward from there.

How do all these benefits occur?

As you read further about the components of a balanced literacy approach, you will see where these benefits appear in your daily plans. First, let's look at the reading components and how they fit into a Reading Workshop. Then we'll focus on the writing components as they look in a Writing Workshop.

This is a turtle shell.

Daily Balanced Literacy Schedule

As you plan your daily schedule, try to allocate at least an hour to **both** the Reading and Writing Workshop portions of your day. The following is a sample of how you might use your workshop time.

5-10 minutes:	Warming Up Activities
15-30 minutes:	Whole-group Instruction
30-50 minutes:	Small-group Instruction
10-15 minutes:	Whole-group Instruction/Sharing Time

*Time will vary according to the length of your school day.

Literacy Centers

Literacy Centers: What, Why, and How?

What are literacy centers?

Literacy centers are places in your classroom that provide a wide variety of learning opportunities for children. They allow for many of Cambourne's Conditions of Learning to be present in your classroom. In addition, they provide you with many opportunities to informally assess children. Literacy centers are often incorporated into Reading Workshop time.

What literacy centers should I have in my classroom?

If you were to talk to ten different primary teachers, you may get ten different answers to that question. Here are the basics that you may want to include. The following literacy centers will give children many opportunities to develop their literacy skills.

The Library Corner:  This center can be in any corner of the room where children can choose a good book and curl up to read it. The corner should be an inviting place to read. Here children are immersed through the many opportunities they have to read new books and reread familiar books. The responsibility and practice in selecting one's own books to read helps children to develop into independent readers.

The Listening Lab: In this center, children have the opportunity to follow along and listen to books that are read aloud on audiotapes or CDs. The opportunity to follow along and listen to fluent, expressive readers allows children to develop language skills and their own expression and fluency. Don't be surprised if you hear children imitating the voice of the reader when they read a book which they have listened to previously.

Read the Room: This center encompasses the walls and other physical elements of your classroom. It gives children the opportunity to become familiar with their environmental print as they read texts found around the room.

Word Zone: The Word Zone is a great place for children to play with language through manipulative tasks. Children can sort, match, read, and write letters and words as they begin to develop their proficiency in letter and word recognition.

The Writing Center: In this center, children are involved in lots of writing opportunities. They can respond thoughtfully to books they have read, enhancing their comprehension. They can also develop their abilities to express themselves through print. Composing letters, stories, poems, and so much more helps children to see the power of printed language.

The Artist's Studio: Here is the place where artists express themselves through art and writing about their art. Children nurture their imaginations as they create art and respond to books they've read.

Why should my classroom include literacy centers?

One of the most important reasons to include literacy centers in your classroom is that they provide one of the most joyful times of the day–when children are truly engaged in their learning! That's not the only reason though. When literacy centers are set up with careful thought, they . . .

- provide many opportunities to meet the conditions of learning.
- allow for learning that is meaningful and relevant to a child's life as a student.
- accommodate a variety of learning styles.
- provide time for teachers to observe children.
- allow children to approximate their reading and writing skills.
- provide opportunities for children to be responsible learners.
- allow children to use their knowledge and practice literacy skills and strategies.
- provide a social atmosphere for children.
- provide opportunities to celebrate children's accomplishments with their classmates and their teacher.

How do I make sure that my literacy centers provide the most benefits for the children in my classroom?

See pages 64-65 for a planning grid for literacy centers. You can use it to assess which of the Conditions of Learning are present in each center and how those conditions are being met. As you plan your literacy centers, use this grid to make sure you are meeting as many Conditions of Learning as possible.

How do I find the time to set up literacy centers in my classroom?

As educators, our daily schedules are hectic already. The tasks we must accomplish in one day are too numerous to list. It is extremely important for our literacy centers to be easy to set up and easy to maintain throughout the school year. We want to feel successful with centers, and we want children to feel successful. SIMPLICITY is the key!

At the start of the school year, choose two centers with which to begin. The Library Corner and the Listening Lab are good choices. Introduce children to these centers first, adding Read the Room, the Writing Center, Word Zone, and the Artist's Studio later on in the school year.

Suggested Time Line for Introducing Literacy Center

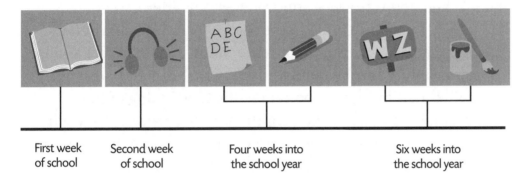

First week of school

Second week of school

Four weeks into the school year

Six weeks into the school year

How do I find space for centers?

For many teachers, the classroom is already a small space for such a large body of learners, so explore ways to accommodate centers with available space. Here are some creative ways to find space in your classroom for centers.

- The tops of cabinets or bookshelves can provide a space for children to work. Some children find sitting in a chair difficult to do for very long so an active center such as Word Zone can easily be done with children standing around a bookshelf that is at an appropriate height for them.

- Create designated center spaces on the floor by hanging a center sign from the ceiling designating that floor space for a particular center. Or lay a tablecloth or piece of fabric on the floor to create a designated area.

- Group children's desks into groups of four or six, creating a natural table for children. If you have tables instead of desks, you can make use of those. Organize supplies for the centers into baskets or other containers, and remove supplies when center time is over.

Do I get children involved in setting up centers?

YES! When you introduce children to a new literacy center, make sure they participate in the setup. Including children in the physical act of setting up a center allows them to feel a sense of responsibility for the maintenance of that center. It also tells them that their input is important to the functioning of the classroom. When you include children in this process, they will take ownership of the centers and of the classroom. In addition, when new children join the class throughout the year, they are surrounded by a support system of peers who truly understand the meaning and the function of each center.

Another benefit of involving children in the setup of centers is that you can talk them through the actual use of that center. You can begin to set expectations for them so when they are working on their own in centers, they know what is expected of them.

Artist's Studio

What kinds of activities can I include in each center throughout the year?

Whatever the activity, remember *simplicity* is important. Center activities should be ongoing and easy to maintain from day to day, week to week, and month to month. As you begin using literacy centers in your classroom, you will find lots activities to engage children in these centers. Suggested materials for your centers, ways to set up your centers, and further information on activities that might take place in each center are provided on pages 31-57. As you plan your literacy centers, keep in mind the Conditions of Learning that are present at each center. The planning grid on pages 64-65 will help you assess how the activities at each center reflect the Conditions of Learning.

When do I allow children time to work at these literacy centers?

You can use the literacy centers in your classroom while you are working with individuals or small groups of children. Literacy centers allow children to be involved in reading and writing activities, even though you are not directly working with them.

Will kindergartners be able to move through the centers independently?

Working in groups independent from the teacher can be challenging for children at any level, but kindergartners can certainly learn to handle this challenge. Your children will need lots of support in the beginning of the year when literacy centers are new to them. It is important to model the kinds of behavior and learning experiences you expect from children in literacy centers. You may consider asking several parent volunteers to monitor centers until the children are comfortable with what is expected of them during this time. Parent volunteers can answer questions and provide guidance while you work with guided reading groups. As the year progresses, you will find that your children are working through centers much more independently.

How do I manage literacy centers?

Management is a personal issue that varies from year to year based on the needs of the children. On pages 58-63 of this book are a variety of management ideas from which to choose. Keep in mind that you will want to adapt these management ideas to meet the needs of your classroom. There is no right or wrong way to manage centers. The most important thing to keep in mind is that all children should have access to all the centers at some point during the week. If you choose a management system that allows children to make decisions about which centers they visit each day, make sure that they do indeed visit a variety of centers within the week instead of working at only two or three of their favorites.

NOTE: As children are involved in small-group shared or guided reading sessions, they may miss one of their center time slots.

The Library Corner

This center is probably the easiest of the centers to manage. After setting out your initial baskets or crates of books, you will want to add and remove material on a periodic basis. Assess your children's needs to determine how often to replace the books. A good rule of thumb is to change the books once a month. This allows you to keep books current with the season or monthly holidays and/or to connect with other curriculum areas such as science and social studies.

As you put new books in the Library Corner introduce them to children. Talk about how you have organized the baskets. For example say, *This basket has all sorts of books about winter.* Children can help you decide which book baskets might be put away. Allowing them to help with this decision gives you the opportunity to gauge their interest levels. If the books about zoo animals have been out for a month, but children still expressed interest in those books, leave them out for another month. Allowing children the opportunity to revisit familiar books leads to fluency and expression.

If you purchase books from a book club, introduce these new books to children when they arrive. Take a few minutes to do a short book talk about several of the books you ordered. These books are a great addition to a "Spotlight Books" basket.

If you have chosen a Big Book to use for your shared reading time for several weeks, gather other books that connect with the theme or topic of the Big Book. These books can be added to a changing basket titled "Big Book Buddies."

As you look at the books provided in your Library Corner, make sure there are a variety of genres and text types available

to read. Think about including the following kinds of printed materials for children to read:

- poetry books

- fiction books that cover a variety of genres such as fairy tales, traditional tales, humor, realistic fiction, fantasy, and so on

- nonfiction books that cover a variety of text types such as how-to, narratives, informational texts, and so on

- easy-to-read books

- age-appropriate encyclopedias

- picture dictionaries

- children's magazines

- age-appropriate newspaper sections such as the cartoon section

Suggested Materials for the Library Corner:

- baskets of books sorted by topics or themes

- pillows

- animal figures or stuffed animals

- furniture conducive to reading such as a rocking chair or bean bag chair

- rug remnants, particularly if your classroom floor is a hard one

Setting Up and Introducing the Library Corner:

1. Tell children that they are going to help you set up a corner in the classroom where they can curl up with a good book to read. Share your thoughts about where you like to read at home and what you think a good reading corner needs like good light, comfortable spaces to read, and so on.

2. Ask children to share where they like to read at home and what they think a good reading corner needs.

3. With the children, choose a corner of your classroom to make into the Library Corner. Ask them to help you arrange pillows and stuffed animals, rug remnants, a rocking chair, beanbag chairs, or whatever furniture you can provide to make the Library Corner an inviting and comfortable place to read.

4. Discuss the kinds of books children like to read. Use their input to decide on the kinds of books with which to stock your library. Do not put out every book you own. Instead, start with a few crates or baskets of books.

5. Point out the different kinds of books you have in each crate or basket. To help children easily find books they are interested in, organize the books by themes or topics. As the year goes on and children express interest in other kinds of books or the class is studying a new theme or topic, add baskets of books to the Library Corner. Remove books on topics or themes that are no longer current.

6. With the children, discuss and decide on rules for using the Library Corner. Remember a few general rules can cover a lot of ground, and children are more likely to remember them if they helped decide on them. Write the rules on a piece of chart paper and post them in the Library Corner as a reminder. Rules might include:

Library Corner Rules

1. Whisper when you are in the Library Corner.

2. Take care of the books you read. Treat them gently as if they belong to you.

3. You may read by yourself, with a friend, or with a stuffed animal.

4. Put books back into the right book baskets.

The Listening Lab

This center is also very easy to maintain throughout the school year. Rotate the audiotapes or CDs from time to time. It's important to make sure that all the children in the classroom have ample opportunity to listen to these audiotapes or CDs at least once or twice before changing them. It is equally important to make sure that children do not become bored by the audiotape or CD that is in the Listening Lab.

In general, you will want to change the materials in the Listening Lab approximately every two to three weeks. This allows children the opportunity to become familiar with the book and its accompanying audiotape or CD.

Ask yourself the following questions as you build your Listening Lab library:

- Do I have a variety of books with audiotapes/CDs? Do I have poetry readings, books with songs, fiction books, and nonfiction books?

- Is the reader engaging and fun to listen to?

- Is the text read at an age-appropriate pace?

- Does the text have any repetition in it, that allows children to join in the reading?

- Is the text appropriate in print size and amount?

Suggested Materials for the Listening Lab:

- cassette or CD player

- headphones

- books with accompanying audiotapes or CDs

- pillows or rug remnants to make the center comfortable to read in OR a table and chairs

Setting Up and Introducing the Listening Lab:

1. Explain that the Listening Lab is a great place for children to listen to books on audiotapes or CDs.

2. Demonstrate use of the audio equipment. It is often helpful to put a red sticker on the STOP button, a green sticker on the PLAY button, and an arrow on the REWIND button to help children distinguish between the operating buttons.

3. Invite children to help you decide where the Listening Lab should be located in the room. Then invite them to help you get the center set up.

4. Introduce one book and its accompanying audiotape or CD. Demonstrate how to turn the pages in the book as you follow along with the audio reading.

5. As the year progresses, you may want to offer several book choices for children. Keep the choices to a minimum. If you offer several choices, put each book and its audiotape or CD in a plastic self-closing bag for storage. This will help children keep the Listening Lab organized.

6. With children, discuss and decide upon the rules for the Listening Lab. Rules might include:

Listening Lab Rules

1. Only a certain number of children can be in the Listening Lab at one time

2. Keep the volume on the cassette or CD player at a low level so only you can hear the book.

3. Use a whisper voice when you follow along with the reader on the audiotape or CD.

4. Put the book and its tape or CD back in the proper storage bag.

Read the Room

This center can be loads of fun for children and teachers alike. There are so many possibilities for activities because this center encompasses your entire classroom. Immersion in print, understanding concepts about print, and recognizing environmental print are three important developmental outcomes of this center.

As children read the room, they can read anything that hangs on the wall or in a pocket chart. As part of this center, set up a place to hang poetry charts or Big Books for children to read. A garment rack makes a great place to hang these types of items. Trouser hangers help make for easy hanging of poetry charts or Big Books. Children can easily take these down, lay them on the floor, and read them.

One way to introduce the Read the Room center is to take a picture of each child in your classroom. Mount each photo to construction paper. Write the names underneath the photos. Then encourage children to read the names of their classmates on the walls of the classroom.

Another exciting addition to Read the Room is a *free writing wall*. Take a large piece of butcher paper and hang it on the wall. Invite children to write their names and draw a self-portrait on this paper. As the year progresses, this free writing wall can be replaced with seasonal or thematic writing and art.

Read the Room objectives can tie into your weekly literacy skill objectives. As you talk about a literacy skill during shared or guided reading sessions, ask children to look for examples of that skill as they read the room. For example, if the week's shared reading focus is the differentiation between capital letters and lowercase letters, ask children to find five examples of uppercase letters and five examples of lowercase letters as they read the room. Here are some other ways you might connect your reading sessions to this literacy center:

- Look for the letters in your name.

- Look for words that start with the same letter as your name or a friend's name.

- Look for words that have one letter, two letters, three letters, four letters or more.

- Look for a chart that has a diagram on it.

- Tell a friend about a picture on the wall.

- Look for a word that is one syllable (one clap) long, two syllables long, and so on.

- Look for high-frequency words such as *stop, go, and, the,* and so on.

- Look for words that rhyme.

- Look for words that go with a season or a theme being studied.

Suggested Materials for Read the Room:

- Rhyme charts

- Word family charts

- Stories or poems on sentence strips in pocket charts

- Big Books

- Posters that teach concept words such as color words, days of the week words, weather words, cross-curricular subjects, and so on.

- Teacher or children's artwork or writing

- Pointers such as dowel rods or unsharpened pencils

Setting Up and Introducing Read the Room:

Once you have some items with print on your walls, tell children, *I am going to read the room.* Ask them to follow quietly behind you. It is helpful if you hang things at the children's eye level so they can easily follow the print.

As you walk around the room, use a pointer to indicate the words and read aloud several charts on the walls. Explain that this center encompasses the entire room.

Invite volunteers to read several charts in the room. If children read incorrectly, gently point out the correct way to read it, and praise them for their effort whether they were accurate or not. The object of this kind of center is to immerse children in print and help them attend to that print.

Help children set rules for this center. This is particularly important so as to keep those that are reading the room on task while not disturbing others. Rules might include:

Read the Room Rules

1. Walk slowly and quietly around the room.

2. Only use pointers to indicate to the words on the wall.

3. Read the room in a whisper voice.

4. Only a certain number of children can read the room at one time.

As the year progresses, change the charts on your walls. Always take time to read new charts with children. Invite them to help you decide what to put up on the walls. Children will be more engaged in reading the room if they have a say in the items that are displayed there.

Helpful Hints:

For safety purposes, think carefully about the pointers children use. The following items work well as pointers:

- Dowel rods cut to a length of not more than 18-inches long. Put a small rubber eraser on one end of the dowel rod.

- Rulers. They are readily available in most classrooms.

The Writing Center

The Writing Center will evolve throughout the year. At the beginning of the year, keep the activities simple. When children enter kindergarten, some will have had experiences writing notes to parents or making play grocery lists. These are wonderful experiences to build on. Encourage approximation as children begin experimenting with writing their thoughts on paper.

Provide a variety of paper media for children to write upon. These might include postcards, stationery, note cards, construction paper, white copy paper, sticky notes, and so on. As the year progresses, add pre-made blank books in a variety of sizes to encourage children to begin writing stories. These pre-made books are easy to make. Simply fold some paper in half and staple along the sides. If you can, visit a local decorating store and ask for their old wallpaper books. The wallpaper samples make great covers for student books.

Suggested Materials for the Writing Center:

- a variety of papers, cards, postcards, envelopes

- pencils, colored pencils, markers, crayons, and yarn

- transparent tape, stapler, three-hole punch

- pre-made blank books

- baskets or containers in which to organize supplies

Setting Up and Introducing the Writing Center:

1. Talk about what it means to be a writer. Share your thoughts about this while encouraging children to share theirs.

2. Ask children what kinds of supplies they might need in a writing center. Gather some of the materials and invite children to help you organize them in the center. As you set up the center, demonstrate how children can make their own books using of some of the supplies such as the transparent tape, the stapler, and the three-hole punch.

3. Brainstorm types of writing children might choose to do in this center. Get the brainstorming activity started by talking about the kinds of writing you do every day such as notes to other teachers, grocery lists, or letters to friends. Write the list on a piece of chart paper to hang in the center. Children can refer to this list as they work in the center. New types of writing can be added as the year progresses.

4. With the children, discuss and decide upon the rules for the Writing Center. Rules might include:

Writing Center Rules

1. Use a whisper voice when working in the center.
2. Use only the supplies you need.
3. After you finish using supplies, put them back where they belong.
4. Write your name on all pieces of your writing.

Types of Writing

Encourage children to try the following types of writing as they use the Writing Center throughout the school year.

- ABC books, 1-2-3 books, and colors books

- letters to friends or family members

- lists such as "to do" lists, wish lists, and so on

- step-by-step directions on how to do something

- poems

- *All About Me* books

- a book of favorites

- diary/journal entries (can include both personal diary entries and observation journal entries)

Word Zone

This center allows children to play with language. By sorting, matching, and writing letters and words, children can begin to develop their knowledge of both letters and high-frequency words. Playing with letters and words allows children to develop their vocabulary, also.

At the start of the kindergarten year, begin with simple tasks in the Word Zone. The following are great Word Zone activities for the start of the school year:

- match capital letters

- match lowercase letters

- match the capital letter to its lowercase letter

- make your first name using magnetic letters (or foam letters)

- practice writing your name on a dry erase board

- put the capital letters in ABC order

- put the lowercase letters in ABC order

- write the alphabet on a dry erase board

As the year progresses, you can incorporate many other literacy skills in this center. Look to your shared and guided reading sessions for ideas about activities. The following activities might be included as the year progresses.

- Label three lunch bags or other small containers with three different word families such as *bat, pet,* and *sit.* Then provide index cards with other words that belong in each of those word families. Children can sort the word cards into the appropriate

containers. See Appendix A on pages 149-151 for word family cards. Common rimes that might be used in making word family cards include:

ay	ill	ip	at	am	ag	ack	ank	ick	ell
ot	ing	ap	unk	ail	ain	eed	oy		out	ug
op	in	an	est	ink	ow	ew	ore	ed	ab
ob	ock	ake	ine	ight	im	uck	um		

- Using photographs of the children in your class, make name cards that have both a child's picture and name written on them. Children can pick a name card out of a basket and then spell the name using magnetic or foam letters or letter tiles, or they can write the name on a dry erase board.

- Create picture cards that represent word families. For example, create picture cards for *dog, log,* and *frog.* Underneath each picture, write the name of the object. Children can sort the picture cards by words that rhyme. They can practice spelling the words using magnetic or foam letters or letter tiles, or they can write them on a dry erase board. See Appendix A on pages 149-151 for word family cards.

- Create picture cards that represent singular and plural objects. Write the words underneath each picture. (Use objects where the plural is spelled by simply adding an *s* to the end.) Children can pair up the singular cards with their plural counterparts. Children can practice making the singular word and then make the plural word with magnetic or foam letters or letter tiles. See Appendix B on pages 152-155 for singular/plural cards.

- During shared reading sessions, you may point out high-frequency words to children, such as *I, me, the, see, for, like,* and so on. Help children become familiar with these words with high-frequency word activities in the Word Zone. Introduce a word in your shared reading session. Reinforce that word in guided reading sessions. Show children how to write the word during a modeled writing session, and then encourage them to make the word as quickly as they can using magnetic or foam letters or letter tiles in the Word Zone. See Appendix C on pages 156-163 for high-frequency word cards.

- Introduce letter sounds in your shared reading sessions. Reinforce the sounds in guided reading sessions. Show children how to write words that begin with those sounds during modeled writing sessions and encourage them to make words with those beginning sounds in the Word Zone.

- Using children's name cards or high-frequency word cards, have children sort the cards by the way they start. Extend this activity by having children sort the words that have an *a* in them and those that don't, or words that have four letters and those that don't, and so on. See Appendix C on pages 156-163 for high-frequency word cards.

Suggested Materials for the Word Zone:

- magnetic letters
- cookie sheets (check to make sure they are magnetic)
- foam letters
- letter tiles
- word/letter cards (See Appendices A, B, C, E)
- small dry erase boards and dry erase markers
- ABC blocks
- magic slates or other reusable writing surfaces
- baskets or other containers to organize supplies

Setting Up and Introducing the Word Zone:

1. Gather children into a large circle on the floor. Brainstorm words that they can read. Ask children where they might see these words–on signs, mail, cereal boxes, and so on.

2. Give each child a few magnetic letters. Ask children to identify the letters. Help those that are unsure of the letters.

3. Hold up a high-frequency word card, reading it aloud. Then ask children who have letters in that word to put their letters in the middle of the circle. Model how to make the high-frequency word using the magnetic letters. Explain that this is just one of the activities they can do in the Word Zone. When first introducing this center, demonstrate only one or two activities that children may engage in while at the Word Zone.

4. Explain the purpose of the Word Zone to children–to practice identifying letters, sorting and matching letters and words, and making words with a variety of materials.

5. Invite children to help you organize the magnetic and foam letters for this center. By allowing them to help organize the center's supplies, children are more likely to remember the organizational system.

Helpful Hints:

Organize magnetic letters on large cookie sheets or in plastic containers with compartments, such as a tackle box. Have children sort the capital letters in ABC order on one cookie sheet and the lowercase letters on another sheet.

The Artist's Studio

Creative expression is an important vehicle for children to use as they reflect on the literature they have been exposed to through read alouds, shared reading sessions, or guided reading experiences. The way children respond creatively to a piece of literature can tell a lot about how they interpreted or comprehended that piece of text.

When children draw, paint, or create, their masterpieces can provide an opportunity for writing experiences to follow. As children create their artwork, it's important to ask them to talk and/or write about what they have created. A child's illustration may be the start of an entire story.

At the start of the school year keep supplies in the Artist's Studio to a minimum. Do not overwhelm children with choices of artistic media. Stock the center with simple supplies such as markers, crayons, and colored pencils. As the year progresses, add other artistic mediums such as watercolor paints, finger paints, and tempera paint.

Helpful Hints:

Limit supplies to one type of paint at a time to keep clean up easier.

The list of activities for the Artist's Studio is endless. Keep the activities as open-ended as possible. Keep essential supplies on hand so children can choose what they need to create their art. Providing art projects to be completed makes the Artist's Studio a high-maintenance center. So keep it simple! Here are a few ways to connect this center to read alouds, shared reading sessions, or guided reading experiences:

- Ask children to draw their favorite part of a story. Encourage them to then write a sentence or two about that part of the story.

- Have children draw something that happened at the beginning, in the middle, and at the end of the story. Invite them to retell the story using the pictures they drew.

- As a whole class, have the children create a mural that depicts the main topic or theme of a book. This works well for non-fiction books. For example, if a read aloud was about different kinds of healthy foods, children might draw these healthy foods on a mural. Then they can label their drawings. This mural can be revisited and read as part of the Read the Room center.

- Ask children to illustrate various concepts learned during a reading experience. For example, have children illustrate positional words such as *up/down, out/in,* and so on.

- Invite children to illustrate their versions of a popular poem, nursery rhyme, or simple patterned book.

- Have children draw or paint a picture of themselves. Invite them to write about something they like to do and something they don't like to do. This is a great beginning of the year project so each member of the class can learn something about his or her classmates.

Suggested Materials for the Artist's Studio:

- easel or work table

- newspaper or a plastic floor covering (A plastic coated tablecloth works great.)

- a variety of paper for drawing and painting

- pencils, colored pencils, markers, crayons, watercolors, poster paints, finger paints

- scissors, hole punches

- glue, transparent tape

- yarn, buttons, fabric scraps, and other odds and ends

- baskets or other containers in which to organize supplies

- clean-up supplies such as rags, sponges, paper towels

Setting Up and Introducing the Artist's Studio:

1. If children have artwork already displayed in the classroom, talk about it. Use this discussion as a springboard for introducing children to the Artist's Studio. You might also ask children to find a book in the Library Corner that has illustrations in it that they enjoy. Talk about the importance of artwork as an enhancement to writing.

2. Invite children to name things artists need in their artists' studios. As children name supplies that you have available for them to use, ask volunteers to set those supplies in the Artist's Studio. Once again, allowing children to name the supplies and help set up the center creates ownership of that center.

3. Demonstrate how you, as an artist, draw or paint a picture and then write about it. Your written account can be in the form of labels, a sentence or two, or a short story. As the year progresses, you may model more sophisticated drawings or paintings along with more sophisticated written accounts.

4. This center will require a lot of discussion about the procedures for using it. Be sure to set clear procedures with children so when clean up time begins, children know exactly what is expected of them. Procedures might include:

Artist's Studio Rules

1. Only a certain number of children at the Artist's Studio at one time.

2. Cover all surfaces with newspaper before painting.

3. Put the caps/covers back on markers and paints.

4. Clean up any spills right away.

Helpful Hints:

Use one type of paint at a time in the center. Demonstrate how to use each type of paint medium properly, include cleaning up the supplies when finished.

Thematic Center Ideas

Center activities can be set up to piggyback off of the shared reading texts, or they can be set up based on a theme you are studying in your classroom. The following pages share some center ideas for popular thematic units:

- Down on the Farm

- Animals, Animals Everywhere

- Colors and Shapes

- Sensational Seasons

Remember, even if your centers are theme-based, the main focus should continue to be on reading and writing strategies and skill work.

Down on the Farm

The Library Corner:

Chitwood, Suzanne Tanner. *Wake Up, Big Barn.* New York, NY: Cartwheel Books, 2002.

Cowley, Joy. *Mrs. Wishy-Washy.* New York, NY: Philomel Books, 1999.

Hillenbrand, Will. *Fiddle-I-Fee.* New York, NY: Gulliver Books, 2002.

Lesser, Carolyn. *What a Wonderful Day to Be a Cow.* New York, NY: Dragonfly, 1999.

The Listening Lab:

Shaw, Nancy. *Sheep in a Jeep.* Boston, MA: Houghton Mifflin, 1999.

Brown, Margaret Wise. *Big Red Barn.* New York, NY: Harper Audio, 1998.

Lindberg, Reeve. *The Midnight Farm.* New York, NY: Weston Woods Studio, 1980.

The Writing Center:

- Have children make a list of the animals that they would have on their farm.

- Invite children to write to a local farmer and ask him or her questions about the animals or the farm.

- Encourage children to write poems about their favorite farm animals.

The Artist's Studio:

- Have children draw or paint a picture of their favorite farm animals. Encourage them to label their pictures or write a sentence about them.

- Invite children to draw a map that shows where everything is located on their imaginary farm.

- Have children create a farm mural to hang on the classroom wall. Label the animals, farm machinery, crops, and so on.

Word Zone:

- Create farm animal picture cards that are labeled. Then ask children to use magnetic letters to recreate the name of the animals. Animals might include: *cow, cat, dog, frog, hen, pig, horse, sheep.* These cards can also be used to play a memory and matching game.

- Have children write a list of words that rhyme with *cat, dog, hen,* and *pig.*

- Have children think of words that start like *farmer, horse, cow,* and *pig.*

Read the Room:

- Hang the words to the song "Old MacDonald Had a Farm" on the wall for children to read. You might use pictures as reminders of the different animals. You might also hang farm poetry or nursery rhymes that relate to the farm around the room for children to read, for example, "Little Boy Blue," "Little Bo Peep," "To Market, To Market," "Mary Had a Little Lamb," and so on.

- Invite children to read the labels for the farm mural created in the Artist's Studio.

- Hang photos of farm animals around the room. Label each photo with a sentence that says, *I am a _____. I say _____.* For example, *I am a dog. I say woof.* Invite children to read about each of the animals.

Animals, Animals Everywhere

Library Corner:

Carle, Eric. *The Very Hungry Caterpillar.* New York, NY: Putnam, 1984.

Wadsworth, Olive. *Over in the Meadow.* New York, NY: North South Books, 2002.

Lawrence, John. *This Little Chick.* Cambridge, MA: Candlewick Press, 2002.

Andreae, Giles. *Giraffes Can't Dance. New York, NY:* Orchard Books, 2001.

Listening Lab:

Rey, H.A. *Curious George Visits the Zoo.* Boston, MA: Houghton Mifflin Audio, 1988.

Pfeffer, Wendy. *From Tadpole to Frog.* New York, NY: Harper Audio, 1996.

Brett, Jan. *Annie and the Wild Animals.* Boston, MA: Houghton Mifflin Audio, 1999.

Weeks, Sarah. *Follow the Moon.* New York, NY: HarperCollins Juvenile Books, 1995.

Writing Center:

- Have children write about their favorite animals. Encourage them to describe their animals and to tell where they live.

- Invite children to write letters to a zookeeper, asking questions about how to care for their favorite animals.

- Encourage children to write a story about animals. They might write a humorous story about what would happen if they brought an elephant home from the zoo, a realistic story about pets they have at home, or a report including animal facts.

Artist's Studio:

- Invite children to draw or paint pictures of their favorite animals. Encourage children to draw their animals in a realistic habitat.

- Have children illustrate the stories they wrote in the Writing Center.

- Invite the class to create a mural of a zoo. Children can paint or draw animals and label them.

Word Zone:

- Label six brown paper bags with animal names such as *zebra, tiger, lion, giraffe, bear, seal*. Include pictures of these animals on the bags. Then create other picture cards with the same beginning sounds–be sure to label each picture–and ask children to sort the picture cards by beginning sounds.

- Create a simple word find with animal names in it. List the animal names with simple pictures next to the names. Be sure that animal names are found going across from left to right. Kindergarten children are not ready to see words up and down, backwards, or on a diagonal yet.

- Ask children to create as many words as possible that rhyme with several animal names such as *dog* and *cat*. They can use letter tiles or magnetic letters or write their words on a dry erase board.

Read the Room:

- Hang animal poetry around the classroom. Be sure to introduce this poetry during read aloud or shared reading times.

- Invite children to read the names of the animals listed on alphabet charts you may have hanging in the room. Many commercial alphabet charts list animals as representatives of the letters.

- Encourage children to read the labels on their zoo mural which was created in the Artist's Studio.

Colors and Shapes

The Library Corner:

Seuss, Dr. *My Many Colored Days*. Westminster, MD: Knopf, 1998.
Heller, Ruth. *Color.* New York, NY: Puffin, 1999.
Hoban, Tana. *Shapes, Shapes, Shapes.* New York, NY: William Morrow and Company, 1986.
MacDonald, Suse. *Sea Shapes.* New York, NY: Voyager Picture Books, 1998.

The Listening Lab:

Peek, Merle. *Mary Wore Her Red Dress and Henry Wore His Green Sneakers*. New York, NY: Clarion Books, 1993.
Caudle, Brad, et al. *Colors, Shapes and Counting*. Conroe, TX: Rock N Learn, 1995.
Thompson, Kim. *Colors & Shapes*. Akron, OH: Twin Sisters Productions, 1997.

The Writing Center:

- Invite children to make a list of things that are a particular color or a particular shape. These lists could be collected and combined into a *Colors and Shapes* book.

- Have children write about the colors they see when they look out the window at school. For example, *I see the green grass. I see the yellow slide.*

- Encourage children to write poetry about colors or shapes. You might encourage them to create their own version of "Roses are Red, Violets are Blue." For example:

> The sun is yellow,
> The sky is blue,
> A pyramid is a triangle,
> And this piece of cheese is, too.

The Artist's Studio:

- Encourage children to experiment with colors. Invite children to mix finger paints or watercolors to get different colors.

- Challenge children to draw pictures that use only the following shapes: triangle, circle, and square.

- Invite children to illustrate the *Colors and Shapes* book that they made in the Writing Center.

Word Zone:

- Create a set of memory and matching game cards that have basic colors listed on them. Invite children to play the game. They may use their crayons to help them read the colors on the cards.

- Focus children's attention on several consonant blends at the beginning of color and shape words. Ask them to think of other words that start with those consonant blends. For example, *blouse* starts like *blue*.

- Ask children to put the color words in alphabetical order.

Read the Room:

- Encourage children to read color words and shape words concept posters around the room.

- Using the basic verse from *Mary Wore Her Red Dress and Henry Wore His Green Sneakers*, create sentence strips with children's names and color words. Children can substitute their names and different color words as they sing the basic verse.

- Display poetry that incorporates color or shape words in it. After reading this poetry with children at read aloud or shared reading times, invite them to revisit the poems while reading the room.

Sensational Seasons

The Library Corner:

Gibbons, Gail. *The Reason for Seasons*. Boston, MA: Holiday House, 1996.

Winnick, Karen. *A Year Goes Round: Poems for the Months*. Honesdale, PA: Boyds Mills Press, 2001.

Siddals, Mary McKenna. *Tell Me a Season*. New York, NY: Clarion Books, 1997.

Rylant, Cynthia. *In November*. Orlando, FL: Harcourt, 2000.

The Listening Lab:

Maestro, Betsy. *Why Do Leaves Change Color?* New York, NY: Harper Audio, 1996. (Fall)

Burton, Virginia Lee. *Katie and the Big Snow*. Boston, MA: Houghton Mifflin Audio, 1999. (Winter)

McCloskey, Robert. *Make Way for Ducklings*. New York, NY: Penguin USA, 1993. (Spring)

Garcia, Jerry, et al. *The Teddy Bears' Picnic*. New York, NY: HarperCollins Juvenile Books, 1996. (Summer)

The Writing Center:

- Invite children to write poems about their favorite seasons.

- Have children write stories or make lists about activities they are involved in during the four seasons.

- Encourage children to write a weather report for each of the four seasons. They may want to role-play the TV meteorologist as they share their reports.

The Artist's Studio:

- Have children illustrate a picture of themselves involved in an outside activity during each of the four seasons. Have

children write or dictate a sentence about their pictures. Display the pictures around the room.

- Invite children to create wall murals that represent each of the four seasons.

- Encourage children to show the cycles of trees during the four seasons.

Word Zone:

- Create word banks that are representative of each season. Include simple pictures to help children read the words. Then have children sort the words into the correct seasons. For example, "Winter Words" might include *snow, snowman, cold, windy, ice.*

- Using the same word cards created for the activity above, ask children to sort the cards by the number of letters in each word. They might also sort the cards by beginning or ending letters.

- Encourage children to create their own list of words that represents each season. They can use books that talk about the various seasons, or they can use other references to help them create their list of words.

Read the Room:

- Display poetry that relates to the four seasons. Be sure to read this poetry together during read aloud or shared reading times. Then encourage children to revisit the poetry while they work in this center.

- Create sentence strips that relate to the weather. For example, *It is <u>spring</u>. Today's weather is <u>sunny</u>.* Children can change the underlined portions of the sentence strips by placing the appropriate words in the sentence.

- Using the pictures children drew of themselves in the Artist's Studio, encourage them to read the sentences underneath each picture.

Managing Literacy Centers

Center Management #1: Assigned Groupings Chart

Group children into heterogeneous groupings of no more than six children per group. Groups of four are best. Allow children to decide on a name for their group.

Each day, assign groups to the centers that they are to visit during center time. Each group should know both the centers they are to visit and the order in which they are to visit them. Rotate groups through the centers during the week's rotation.

In this type of management system, the teacher exercises most of the control. This system works well at the start of the year. As the year progresses and children become more independent, you may want to move to another type of management system that allows them to have more choice.

Note: If you use this type of management system for a length of time, it is important to change the groupings of children. Changing the groups allows children to get to know other classmates while learning new things from new situations. Children learn from each other's strengths. Changing the groups every three to four weeks works well.

	Monday	Tuesday	Wednesday	Thursday	Friday
Otters: Chris Maria Juan Kataruna					
Seals: Brad Laura Sasha Ryne					
Penguins: Alexis Brianna Tim Gary					
Turtles: Todd Savannah Franco Tori					
Pelicans: Mark Lee Katacha Arianna					

Center Management #2: Individual Agenda Boards

This management system allows children to create their own agendas, using an agenda board. Each day, children choose two centers to visit. Then they create an agenda listing those centers.

Children's agenda boards can be made out of 8 1/2" x 11" pieces of tagboard, divided into two sections (based on a forty-minute small group session). Each section has a pocket made out of a library pocket card or a small, unsealed envelope. Children choose two center sticks, which can be made out of craft sticks. Each craft stick is labeled with the name of a center. Depending on the number of children in your class, you will want to limit the number of center sticks available for each center. This will prevent individual centers from being over populated.

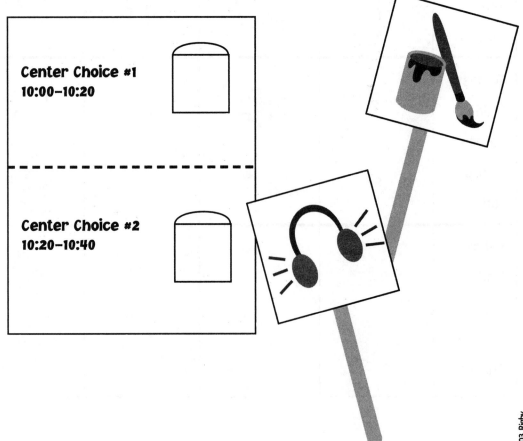

Center Choice #1
10:00–10:20

Center Choice #2
10:20–10:40

Center Management #3: Center Choice Board

This management system is similar to the agenda boards. However, it allows the teacher to see at a glance who is going to which center. (While the agenda board is usually kept with the child or at his or her desk, this board is posted in the room where everyone can easily see it.)

Create a chart with all of the centers listed. Each center needs to have a number of hook and loop fasteners by it. Children each have two name cards, which also have hook and loop fasteners on the back of them. Children put each of their name cards by the centers they choose to visit that day (one name card per time slot). Limiting the number of children that can visit a center at one time allows you to keep a balance of children amongst the centers.

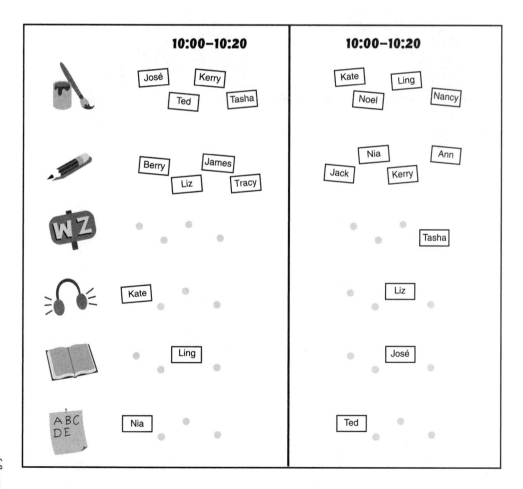

Center Management #4: Accountability System

If you choose a center management system that allows children to pick the centers that they visit each day, you are providing them with the opportunity to practice being responsible learners. When children are told what is expected of them, most are able to assume the responsibility. If you tell children that you expect them to visit different centers each day, most children will adhere to that expectation. However, there are some children who need more guidance. If you find this is the case with children in your classroom, you may want to include this accountability system as a part of your weekly center management.

Each child is given a "Centers I Visited" sheet each week. They then keep track of the centers they visit every day. At the end of the week, you have an easy tracking system for the centers they visited.

Centers I Visited

	Monday	Tuesday	Wednesday	Thursday	Friday

Planning for Literacy Centers

Conditions of Learning			
Immersion			
Expectation			
Responsibility			
Approximation			
Demonstration			
Response			
Use			

Planning for Literacy Centers

Conditions of Learning			
Immersion			
Expectation			
Responsibility			
Approximation			
Demonstration			
Response			
Use			

Balanced Literacy Reading Workshop

As you plan your daily schedule, attempt to plan at least an hour for your Reading Workshop time. The following reading components should be part of your Reading Workshop:

• Modeled Reading/Read Alouds

• Shared Reading

• Guided Reading

• Independent Reading

These components fall into your daily Reading Workshop schedule in the following way:

5-10 minutes: Warming Up Activities (These often consist of revisiting songs, poems, rhymes, rereading of a Big Book, or Modeled Reading/Read Alouds.)

15-30 minutes: Whole-group Instruction (Shared Reading)

30-50 minutes: Small-group Instruction (Guided Reading and literacy centers)

10-15 minutes: Whole-group Instruction/Sharing Time (Modeled Reading/Read Alouds and time for sharing what children have accomplished during literacy centers.)

Modeled Reading/Read Aloud

Reading aloud to children is essential for their literacy development, and it's one of the most enjoyable parts of the day. There are so many outstanding picture books to share with children. Every year, hundreds of new titles line bookstore shelves. So grab a few engaging texts and read aloud to children.

Read alouds should occur at least once a day every day. If your schedule permits, plan read alouds twice a day. Choose a variety of read aloud texts, ranging from captioned text to rhyming text to involved story lines. Read aloud both fiction and nonfiction books. Vary the fiction genres and the nonfiction text types. Choose some read alouds that may be picked up at a later time and read by a child. Choose other read alouds that stretch children's zone of proximal development, providing a bit more sophisticated language or structure than what they might be able to read on their own.

Note: Chapter books are more appropriate read alouds for second grade and up. Primary children need closure to the stories they hear.) Reading aloud is an excellent warming up activity in which to engage children.

As you read aloud, you are modeling for children what a proficient reader does. By adding expression to your voice when appropriate, you are modeling how a reader becomes engaged in a story. You are showing children that reading is not just a matter of reading individual words.

At times, you may stumble over a few words. As a proficient reader, you know to go back and reread. This behavior occurs naturally for us, but children need to see that behavior explicitly modeled. On occasion, you may want to stop and explain what you did–*Oops! That didn't make any sense when I read that. I better go back and try that again,* or *Wow! That's a word I don't know how to pronounce. I need to break it into chunks…Yes, that sounds right. I'll read that sentence again.*

Note: You need not stop every time you make a miscue. Too many interruptions will cause children to lose sight of the whole story's meaning.

As you read aloud, your emotions are often expressed naturally. When you read a funny story, you laugh. On the other hand, when the story is sad, you may sigh or comment on how bad you feel for a character. These natural reactions provide a model for children, showing them how readers become involved in the books they read.

Read Aloud Resources

Archambault, John and Bill Martin, Jr. *Chicka Chicka Boom Boom!* New York, NY: Aladdin Paperbacks, 2000.

Barrett, Judi. *I Knew Two Who Said Moo.* New York, NY: Atheneum, 2000.

Brett, Jan. *Hedgie's Surprise.* New York, NY: Putnam, 2000.

Brett, Jan. *The Mitten. New York, NY:* Putnam, 1996.

Carle, Eric. *The Very Hungry Caterpillar.* New York, NY: Putnam, 1984.

Cherry, Lynne. *The Great Kapok Tree.* Orlando, FL: Voyager Picture Book, 2000.

Delacre, Lulu. *The Message in the Stars*. Barrington, IL: Rigby, 2003.

Dzamtovski, Diane. *The Princess and the Pea*. Barrington, IL: Rigby, 2000.

Ehlert, Lois. *Growing Vegetable Soup*. Orlando, FL: Harcourt, 1987.

Fox, Mem. *Hattie and the Fox*. Glenview, IL: Scott Foresman, 1992.

Gelman, Rita. *More Spaghetti I Say!* Tapeka, KS: Econo-Clad Books, 1999.

Hutchins, Pat. *Rosie's Walk*. Glenview, IL: Scott Foresman, 1983. (wordless book)

Lobel, Anita. *Alison's Zinnia*. Fairfield, NJ: Greenwillow, 1990.

Manners, Jane. *The Wise Woman and the Sky*. Barrington, IL: Rigby, 2000.

Martin, Bill, Jr. *Brown Bear, Brown Bear, What Do You See?* New York, NY: Henry Holt and Co., 1996.

Martin, Bill, Jr. *Polar Bear, Polar Bear, What Do You Hear?* New York, NY: Henry Holt and Co., 1997.

Numeroff, Laura. *If You Give a Moose a Muffin*. Glenview, IL: Scott Foresman, 1991.

Rosen, Michael. *We're Going on a Bear Hunt*. New York, NY: Little Simon, 1997.

Suess, Dr. *The Cat in the Hat*. Westminster, MD: Random House, 1957.

Suess, Dr. *I Am Not Going to Get Up Today!* Westminster, MD: Random House, 1988.

Sweeny, Sheila. *Where Do Elephants Stomp?* Barrington, IL: Rigby, 2003.

Suess, Dr. *One Fish, Two Fish, Red Fish, Blue Fish*. Westminster, MD: Random House, 1981.

Wells, Rosemary. *Timothy Goes to School*. New York, NY: Vikings Childrens Books, 2000.

Williams, Sue. *I Went Walking*. Orlando, FL: Harcourt, 1992.

Wood, Audrey. *Jubal's Wish*. New York, NY: Blue Sky Press, 2000.

Wood, Audrey. *The Napping House*. Orlando, FL: Harcourt, 1984.

Shared Reading

Shared reading was developed to provide children with a bedtime story format in the classroom. (Don Holdaway, 1979.) By using a Big Book or a poetry chart–any text that is enlarged– children gather around to share the experience of reading together.

During the initial reading of a Big Book or other enlarged text, it is your role to model the reading of the text. In subsequent readings, invite children to join in as you read the text. This is where the term *shared reading* comes from. Children are sharing in the responsibility of reading the text. Revisiting and rereading shared reading texts provides great warming up activities.

The Benefits of Shared Reading

The benefits of shared reading are far-reaching. This component of a balanced literacy program. . .

- allows you to demonstrate a variety of comprehension strategies and literacy skills.

- provides an opportunity to teach children concepts about print.

- helps children begin to understand story language.

- builds children's background knowledge on a vast array of topics.

- allows all children to participate at a level at which they feel comfortable.

- builds children's vocabulary.

- allows you to model the three cueing systems: semantic, syntactic, and graphophonic.

- provides an opportunity for discussion about how language works and how text is set up in a variety of genres and nonfiction text types.

- builds children's abilities to make predictions and retell story events.

   The list of benefits is long. Most importantly, children enjoy shared reading. They are able to take risks in a safe environment, and children contribute what they feel they can to a shared reading experience. Much of the reading responsibility rests on the proficient readers shoulders.

   As you choose a text for shared reading, you will want to evaluate it for its many uses. Consider the following points when looking at possible shared reading texts.

What comprehension strategies can you teach?

Perhaps the story has a strong beginning, middle, and end to it. Then demonstrate and focus on the comprehension strategy of synthesizing through a retelling of the story might then be what you would choose to focus on.

What literacy skills can be taught?
If there are numerous characters in the story, you might choose to teach the use of capitalization with names.

What concepts about print that can be taught?
If the text has two or three lines on each page, it provides an opportunity to demonstrate how a proficient reader navigates a return sweep.

Present shared reading session every day. A shared reading session generally lasts twenty to thirty minutes. The shared reading text is often revisited numerous times so new text is not needed everyday. Because of this, it is imperative that the chosen text allows you to teach a variety of different skills and strategies with each revisit. By revisiting shared reading texts frequently over a period of a week or two, children not only get to experience a variety of strategies and skills taught within the context of that text, but they also are able to practice fluency.

Choosing a Big Book

Big Books are available through many markets today; however, not all Big Books are appropriate for use as shared reading books. Almost any story can be produced in a large format, but only some work well for shared reading. Look for the following features when choosing a Big Book to use in your classroom for the purpose of shared reading.

- The amount of text on a page should not be overwhelming to children. You want them to be able to follow along with you as you point to the words.

- The text size should be large enough for children to follow along at a minimal distance.

- The story should be an engaging one.

- The story should have pictures that match and/or add to the text.

- The story should portray familiar experiences.

- The story language should be natural, not contrived.

- The characters should be engaging and memorable for children.

- The text should provide opportunities for children to participate in the reading. This may occur through a recurring phrase, through a cumulative text pattern, or through a rhythm and rhyme pattern.

- The ending should be satisfying for children.

Once you've chosen a Big Book, have fun reading it with the class. Encourage children to read with as you revisit the text from one day to the next. Invite children to revisit the text on their own by placing it either in the Library Corner or as part of the Read the Room center.

Big Book Resources

Barchas, Sarah E. *I Was Walking Down the Road*. New York, NY: Scholastic, 1993.

Cowley, Joy. *Mrs. Wishy-Washy*. Bothell, WA: Wright Group, 1984.

Hutchens, Pat. *Rosie's Walk*. New York, NY: Macmillan, 1968.

Jorgensen, Gail. *Beware*. Barrington, IL: Rigby Education, 1988.

Jorgensen, Gail. *Crocodile Beat*. Barrington, IL: Rigby Education, 1988.

Martin, Jr., Bill *Brown Bear, Brown Bear, What Do You See?* New York, NY: Henry Holt, 1983.

Parkes, Brenda. *The Enormous Watermelon*. Barrington, IL: Rigby Education, 1986.

Parkes, Brenda. *Who's in the Shed?* Barrington, IL: Rigby Education, 1986.

Woody. *I Want My Mom!* Barrington, IL: Rigby Education, 2000.
Zorfass, Judith. *Bella Lost Her Moo*. Barrington, IL: Rigby
Education, 2000.

Other Sources for Shared Reading Texts

As you develop your shared reading lessons, include a variety of texts. Big Books are not always necessary when incorporating shared reading in your balanced literacy program. You can also create your own enlarged print text. Try some of the following ideas to create additional shared reading texts.

- Gather examples of environmental print to read with children.

- Copy nursery rhymes or poetry onto chart paper.

- Copy nursery rhymes or songs onto sentence strips. Place the sentence strips in a pocket chart. Use sentence strips to create additional verses, using children's ideas as a springboard for those new verses.

- Using poster board, write a language experience story with children. Have children illustrate each page (or piece of poster board) and create a "homemade" Big Book.

- Create a class version of a favorite read aloud that has the qualities of an engaging shared reading text. Use poster board or butcher paper to create this enlarged version.

Environmental Print

Environmental print is essential for children to be aware of as they develop their reading and writing skills. Our culture is a print-rich one. Talk about the print that surrounds children everyday. When you make children aware of the print around them, they will become flexible (example: not all lowercase a's look the same), they will begin to see patterns emerge (example: each STOP sign looks the same), and they will begin to understand that print carries a precise message.

Create environmental print cards that can be used as part of shared reading lessons. They may also be incorporated into modeled writing lessons or displayed around the room for children to read during their time in the Read the Room center. Children might also use the cards to play a memory and matching game with environmental print in the Word Zone center.

1. Gather examples of environmental print: fast food restaurant bags and napkins, photographs of local grocery stores and retail stores, photographs of local gas station signs, canned or boxed food labels, candy bar wrappers, coupons, and news paper advertisements.

2. Find pairs of environmental print examples. For example, a coupon for a type of soup and a label from that same soup can be used to create a pair of environmental print cards. Mount these examples on index cards or heavy tagboard and cut into 3 $\frac{1}{2}$" x 5" cards. Laminate the cards for extra durability. Use these cards during shared reading lessons, asking children to read aloud the various environmental print examples. Talk about the features of each sample of environmental print. *What letters appear in the environmental print? What colors? What are the product mascots or icons? Any other identifying features?*

Guided Reading

Guided reading is at the heart of a balanced literacy program. This component takes place in small groups that consist of two to six children. In guided reading, children control their own copies of the guided reading book rather than the teacher having control over one copy of the book as in shared reading. The teacher's role is to guide children through a book that has been carefully chosen to meet their developmental needs. In turn, children are responsible for taking risks as they attempt to read the book.

At the start of the kindergarten year, you may find that few children are ready to take responsibility for reading a text. It is important to make sure that children have had many opportunities to interact with a variety of books, poems, rhymes, and songs in a shared reading environment before they are introduced to guided reading. In particular, children should have sufficient concepts about print before they are given further reading responsibility in a guided reading situation. (See pages 81-85 for more information on concepts about print.) Children should also understand that print carries a message. In addition, some letter recognition, some high-frequency word recognition (including their own name), and the concept that reading should make sense and sound grammatically correct is important for children to understand.

As we group children into guided reading groups, it is important to match children to appropriate books. Looking at the supports and challenges in each chosen book and comparing them to the strengths and weaknesses of the children in the group helps to ensure that children are placed appropriately. It is also important to realize that children progress at their own rates of development. With this in mind, grouping must remain flexible–in other words, children should not be placed in one guided reading group and remain in that group for the rest of the year. Instead constant assessment and evaluation needs to take place. As you see a child moving ahead or falling behind the others in his or her group, you will need to reorganize your groups. It is important to keep children involved in reading books at their instructional levels.

Guided reading books are leveled according to the supports and challenges they provide for readers. There are a variety of leveling systems found in the guided reading market today, so how do you know what level to start a child in? One way to decide where a child should begin is to give him or her three books at three different instructional levels. Ask the child to look at each book and choose one book that seems too hard to read, one book that seems too easy to read, and one book that seems just right to read. This method is sometimes referred to as the "Goldilocks" method. As the child reads this "just right" book, take an oral reading record to assess the child's instructional level. Use the scores and the analysis of the oral reading record to determine the child's placement. (See the Reading Assessment section on pages 94-115 for more information on oral reading records.)

Once children are ready for guided reading, they should be involved in small group instruction three to five times a week. That instruction should generally last around twenty minutes. Guided reading sessions should include:

- Rereading of a familiar guided reading book

- Introduction to a new guided reading book

- Reading of the new text

- Discussion about the text

- Focused instruction of a comprehension strategy or literacy skill

- Response to the guided reading text

Benefits of Guided Reading

The benefits of guided reading as part of your balanced literacy program include:

- Instruction based on children's needs

- The opportunity for children to become increasingly responsible for reading

- The opportunity for children to practice the strategies and skills that were modeled for them in shared reading experiences

- The exploration of a wide variety of fiction genres and nonfiction text types

- The opportunity for teachers to observe children as they problem-solve challenges

Choosing an Appropriate Guided Reading Text

The appropriate text is essential for successful guided reading experiences. The goal of guided reading is to match books to children rather than matching children to books. This ensures that the book a child is reading is supportive, yet stretches him or her to the next level of reading development. When choosing books to match to readers, consider the following.

- Consider the supports and challenges the book offers. Be sure that the book offers many supports with a few challenges to provide children with opportunities to problem-solve and develop new strategies.

- Find books that allow you to practice a particular strategy or skill. If children in one group are having difficulty retelling stories in the correct sequence, then choose a book that has several distinct episodes and can be easily broken down into a beginning, middle, and end for a retelling.

- Look for books that can be read in a short amount of time. Guided reading sessions are short and to the point, so strategies and skills can be talked about promptly.

- Look for books that allow children to experience a variety of fiction genres and nonfiction text types.

Independent Reading

Independent reading is probably the simplest of the reading components to integrate into your daily classroom schedule. Sometimes, however, because of its simplicity we find ourselves thinking that independent reading time is not a useful way to use our precious class time. Think again! The more children are given time to revisit books they can read on their own, the more fluent they will become. Beginning readers must have lots of opportunities to practice reading familiar books. Just like most anything we learn, the more we practice, the better we become. As you plan your daily schedule, build daily independent reading time. At the start of the kindergarten year, independent reading time may only last five minutes. As the year progresses, gradually increase that time. By the end of the year, asking kindergarten children to be involved in at least fifteen minutes of independent reading time is not too much to expect.

Choosing Appropriate Books for Independent Reading

A concern of many teachers regarding independent reading time is that children do not know how to choose appropriate books to read. To help children choose books that are indeed appropriate for them to read during independent reading time, you may want to set up book baskets for each individual child or for a group of children.

You may try to begin each day with children taking care of lunch count and choosing a book from their group's book basket. The books in the basket can be books that children have read in guided reading sessions or that they have seen numerous times in shared reading sessions. (Often you can purchase smaller versions of the Big Books from publishers.) Also include books that children have created themselves. Many of your responses to shared reading books will be to create your own versions of those books.

Tell children that they can choose a few books from their book baskets. The they can choose one other book from the classroom library. This system helps reassure you that children are spending a majority of the independent reading time involved with books that they can read. Independent reading is ineffective when children constantly have their eyes on print that is too difficult for them. They must have the opportunity to read and reread familiar text in order to become fluent readers.

Concepts About Print

As children begin to explore the meaning of print, not only are they trying to figure out what the letters and words say, but they are also trying to understand how print works.

It is important for us to model on a daily basis how print works so children can begin to understand this difficult concept. To us, starting at the left of a page and reading or writing to the right makes perfect sense. In all likelihood, we don't remember a time when print didn't make sense. To children who are just beginning to read and write, all the rules of print seem overwhelming and confusing. So set aside time every day to read to children and engage them in print awareness activities. Listed on the following pages are the concepts about print that you will want to include in your lesson objectives. See the Reading Assessment section for a checklist to assess children's understandings of concepts about print.

- **Identify the front cover.**
  As you read books during read aloud and shared reading sessions, point out the front covers to children. We often assume that this is something they naturally comprehend. In many cases, children do understand the idea of front cover and back cover, thanks to the modeling that happens as we read aloud to them. However, there may be some children who have had few experiences with books before coming to school. In this case, we must make it a point to share this knowledge with them.

- **Identify the title.**
  Whenever you read a book, a newspaper article, a poem, or any other text that has a title, point out the title by saying, *The title of this book is **The Little Red Hen.*** Using book language, or jargon, with children is important.

- **Demonstrate how to hold a book right-side up to read.**
  Once again, this concept seems like a natural one for experienced readers; however, young children often have been known to pick up a book and pretend to read it, all the while holding the book upside down. Be sure to demonstrate how you know the book is right-side up because the letters are right-side up on the cover.

- **Demonstrate how to turn pages.**
  Children may understand the idea of turning pages in a book, but they may not understand when to turn the pages. As you read aloud, share when to turn the page. *I've finished reading the print on this page. To continue reading the story, I have to turn the page.* Then demonstrate that skill.

- **Demonstrate where to begin reading on a page.**
  Shared reading experiences are a good time to demonstrate where to begin reading on a page. Point to the words, being explicit about where you are going to begin reading. This can also be modeled when you demonstrate writing.

- **Demonstrate left-to-right movement.**
  Shared reading experiences are also an appropriate time to demonstrate reading from left to right. Point to the words on the page. Be explicit about the fact that you read from left to right. Show children that you read this word first and then that word next and so on. As you do modeled writing, it is also important to point out that we not only read from left to right, but that we also write from left to right.

- **Demonstrate top-to-bottom movement.**
  Along with demonstrating left-to-right movement, explain that we start at the top of the print and work our way down to the bottom. Once again, this can be demonstrated during shared reading and writing experiences.

- **Demonstrate return sweeps (moving from one line down to the next line).**
  As children approximate reading, they are often unsure of how to move from one line of text to another. So to help children better understand how to attack the challenge of more than one line of print on a page, it is important for you to demonstrate and think aloud about how a reader attacks this challenge. The use of a pointer will help children follow along as you read.

- **Demonstrate the concept of a letter.**
  The term "letter" is jargon that children need to understand. Children may indeed know how to recite the alphabet, thanks to lots of practice at home or in preschool; however, if you ask them to tell you a letter or point to a letter in print, they may not understand what a letter is. During shared reading experiences, it is important to use this term as you talk about the book. You might share things like, *The dog's name is Spot. His name begins with the letter S. Here is the letter S.* As children become more familiar with the term "letter," you may ask them to count the number of letters in their names or in other words. The understanding of a letter precedes the understanding of what makes something a word.

- **Demonstrate the concept of a word.**
  Once again, the term "word" may be unfamiliar to children. They may have heard the term "word" in discussions, but when they look at print they may not understand what constitutes a word. Explain that words are letters put together. Words are separated by spaces. Demonstrate how to count the number of words in a sentence. This activity will help children distinguish between letters and words.

- **Demonstrate the use of critical jargon, such as *first letter, last letter, author,* and *illustrator***
  It is important for beginning readers and writers to understand some of the language we naturally use when we are talking about print. Asking a child to tell you the first letter in a word sounds like an easy task, but if that child doesn't understand the jargon, he or she is unlikely to be successful with that task. As you read and write, be sure to point out these terms to children.

- **Demonstrate one-to-one correspondence.**
  As children develop understandings of letters and words, they will begin to understand one-to-one correspondence. When children begin reading, they often tell the story, not understanding that for every word they say, the text should have a word to match. Both shared reading and shared writing experiences provide opportunities to demonstrate this concept. When children begin guided reading, it is important that they have a good grasp of this concept.

- **Demonstrate the concept of picture/text match.**
  This concept is easily demonstrated and discussed during read alouds and shared reading experiences. Children need to realize that as they read, they can and should look to the pictures to help them understand the text. This concept can also be demonstrated during modeled writing sessions. After writing a sentence or a short story, model how you decide what to draw for a picture.

Sample Lesson: Concepts About Print

1. Engage children in a discussion about the cover of a Big Book.

   - Tell children, as you indicate with your pointer, that the cover of the book tells us the title. *The title is a clue for us. It tells us how to hold the book the right way as we get ready to read.* Point out the author's and the illustrator's names as well.

   - Ask children to share their thoughts about this story based on the cover. *What might this story be about? What makes you think that? So far, does this story remind you of any other stories we have read?*

2. Then walk children through the book, turning the pages and briefly discussing the pictures on each page. Do not read the book to children yet.

3. After talking about the book, go back to the beginning of the book. *Now, let's read the book and see what happens.*

4. As you read, point to each word so children can also attend to the print. Discuss one or two of the following print conventions with each reading:

- Turn one page at a time.
- Always read the left page before reading the right page.
- Begin reading at the left side of the page all the time.
- When you get to the end of a line of text, move down to the next line.
- Begin at the top of the text and read to the bottom of the text.
- Look at the pictures for ideas of what the words say; the print matches the pictures.

5. Return to the Big Book over and over again, each time focusing on a new print convention. As children become familiar with print conventions, ask them to show you the front cover and the title. Ask them where to begin reading and so on.

Phonemic Awareness

Phonemic awareness is critical to literacy development. It is the ability to hear sounds within words. It includes the ability to sequence sounds within words, to segment sounds within words, and to blend sounds together within words. Children develop phonemic awareness through a variety of experiences such as:

- reading experiences with rhymes and poems (Include lots of nursery rhymes in your daily reading activities!)

- singing songs

- participating in oral language experiences

- playing with words

- being involved in print-rich environments

- using inventive spelling in their writing

The following pages have activities that you can use with children to develop their phonemic awareness. These activities are meant to be engaging and fun for children and teachers alike. They can be used as springboards for including phonemic awareness in many of the lessons you teach.

Riddle Me a Rhyme

Enjoy these rhymes with children. Invite them to figure out the answers.

1. This word rhymes with *pig*. A clown wears one on his head. It must be a (*wig*).

2. This word rhymes with *red*. You sleep in one. It must be a (*bed*).

3. This word rhymes with *cat*. A baseball player wears one. It must be a (*hat*).

4. This word rhymes with *look*. We read one everyday. It must be a (*book*).

5. This word rhymes with *pink*. Dirty dishes pile up in it. It must be a (*sink*).

6. This word rhymes with *fox*. We put things in it. It must be a (*box*).

7. This word rhymes with *goat*. It sails on the sea. It must be a (*boat*).

8. This word rhymes with *can*. When a boy grows up, he becomes one. It must be a (*man*).

9. This word rhymes with *fun*. It shines in the sky. It must be the (*sun*).

10. This word rhymes with *star*. I drive in one. It must be a (*car*).

11. This word rhymes with *like*. It has two wheels. It must be a (*bike*).

12. This word rhymes with *might*. We turn it on when it gets dark outside. It must be a (*light*).

13. This word rhymes with *say*. At recess, we do this. It must be (*play*).

14. This word rhymes with *pin*. A fish has two of these. It must be a (*fin*).

15. This word rhymes with *bake*. I like to have one on my birthday. It must be a (*cake*).

Amazing Alliteration

Through the use of alliteration, children can begin to understand the concept of phonemes or beginning sounds. Share these tongue twisters with children and ask them to identify the phoneme that is used over and over in each one. Then write a few of your own silly tongue twisters with the class. Remember to concentrate on the sounds rather than the letters that make those sounds.

Peter Piper picked a peck of pickled peppers.

Sally sells seashells down by the seashore.

Timmy Turtle tucked ten teabags in his teapot.

Bobby bounced his basketball better than Billy.

Fred found four fish for Phil.

Don't dilly dally, Donny.

Yolanda yodels over yummy yogurt.

Henny Hen has the hiccups.

Laura Lou loves lemon lollipops.

My mom makes me mini-muffins.

This Old Man

This popular song is perfect for emphasizing rhyming patterns through oral language fun. Teach children the song and the movements that accompany the song. After singing it together several times, ask children to listen for rhyming words they hear in the song. If need be, model several rhyming examples.

   On chart paper, record pairs of rhyming words children heard in the song. Encourage children to add other rhyming words to the pairs. Add quick line drawings to help children remember what the written words say.

This old man, he played one.
He played knick-knack on my thumb.

Chorus:
With a knick-knack (clap your hands twice), paddy-whack(slap your knees twice),
Give the dog a bone(pretend to give a dog a bone).
This old man came rolling home (roll your hands over each other).

Verses:

Two, shoe	*Seven, till eleven*
Three, knee	*Eight, gate*
Four, door	*Nine, twine*
Five, hive	*Ten, once again*
Six, sticks	

Phonics

Phonics refers to the connections between sound units and their corresponding letters, or sound-symbol recognition. When we read, it is important to keep the use of phonics working alongside the semantic cueing system. Phonics can be a part of your balanced literacy program, taught through the use of Big Books, poems, rhymes, songs, and writing experiences. It is good practice to use every opportunity to incorporate both phonics teaching and phonemic awareness teaching. Although isolated work can be done on particular skills, it should be done using the context of something familiar to children. The following pages contain suggested activities.

NOTE: Be sure that children have had lots of literacy experiences before you begin breaking literacy down into the parts of phonemes and sound-symbol connections.

Going on a Picnic

Sit children in a circle and begin to tell them a story.

We're going on a picnic. Each of us is going to bring along something that starts with the same letter as our first name. Since my first name is Laura, I am going to bring lemonade to our picnic. Here's how I would say it, "L, my name is Laura, and I'm going to bring lemonade." Now it's your turn.

Ask children to each say the letter that starts their first name, followed by their first name, followed by what they will bring to the picnic. As children get more practice with this game, encourage them to say their name and item followed by the previous classmate's name and item.

You can create a classroom book using this game as inspiration. Have children dictate their parts of the story to you. They can then draw a picture of themselves and their items. Collate the pages in ABC order. Add the class book to the Read the Room center or the Library Corner.

Which One Does Not Belong?

In this listening game, list a number of items. Ask children to listen for the item that does not belong. Encourage them to listen for beginning sounds earlier in the year and ending sounds as the year progresses. Encourage children to make connections between the sounds and the letters that make those sounds. Here are some lists to get you started.

boy, ball, cat, bone

purple, bear, pink, pan

dog, fish, dish, day

run, ran, race, win

feet, foot, meet, find

sun, turtle, sand, silly

girl, hand, go, goat

tooth, time, tan, moose

him, her, his, up

van, voice, pop, violin

jump, juice, apple, jelly

yo-yo, no, yes, yellow

kite, kitten, kid, moose

zipper, buttons, zebra, zoo

like, day, love, light

moon, mom, dad, my

nose, net, nice, cat

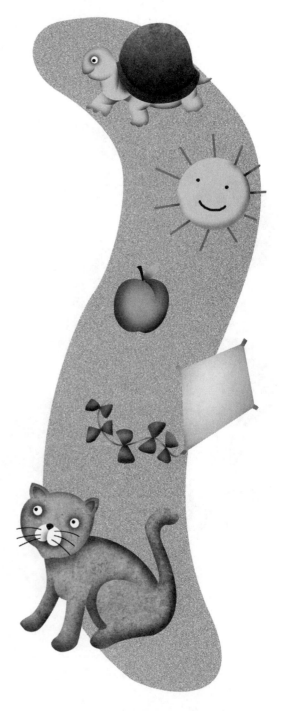

ABC Alphabet Posters

To encourage making connections between letters and sounds, create posters for each letter of the alphabet. Label a piece of tagboard with each letter. Write both the uppercase and lowercase letter on the tagboard.

Invite children to look through old magazines and find five pictures of objects that they know. Have them cut out the pictures. Then have children share the pictures they found. Invite them to tell the beginning sounds they hear for each picture. Children may give you the letter sound or the letter name. Accept both answers and reinforce by repeating what they said while adding the other bit of information. For instance, *Dog does start with /d/ which is what the letter d says.*

Have children glue each picture to the correct letter's poster. Label the pictures so children can see the connections between the beginning letters and their corresponding sounds. Then display these alphabet posters around the room. Children can revisit the posters during their time in the Read the Room center. As children revisit these posters, you might encourage them to look at different posters each day by prompting them. *Look for a picture on our ABC posters that starts with /f/? Find a picture that starts like the word* **ball.** *What sound does it start with? What letter makes that sound?*

Helpful Hint:

For children who have difficulty associating letters and their sounds, try to use classmates names to help them make associations. For instance, **Lettuce** *starts just like* **Laura** *does. They both start with the /l/ sound. They both start with the letter l.*

Reading Assessments

The following reading assessments can be integrated into your balanced literacy classroom. Some of the assessments are informal, such as anecdotal records, while others are more formal, such as oral reading records. If these assessments are new to you, gradually fit them into your assessment repertoire.

Checklists:

Concepts About Print Checklist
Emergent Readers Checklist
Early Readers Checklist
Comprehension Strategies Checklist

Other Assessment Tools:

Anecdotal Records
ABC Knowledge Assessment
Oral Reading Records
Retelling Form

Name:_____ Date:_____

Concepts About Print Checklist

Teacher Directions: During whole-group, small-group, or independent reading time, observe children as they are engaged in the reading process.

Concept	Date of Entry									
Identifies the front cover										
Identifies the title										
Demonstrates how to hold a book right-side up in order to read										
Demonstrates how to turn pages										
Demonstrates where to begin reading on a page										
Demonstrates left-to-right movement										
Demonstrates top-to-bottom movement										
Demonstrates ability to navigate return sweeps (moving from one line of text to the next)										
Demonstrates understanding of a letter										
Demonstrates understanding of a word										
Demonstrates understanding of critical jargon such as *first letter, last letter, author,* and *illustrator*										
Demonstrates understanding of one-to-one correspondence										
Demonstrates understanding of picture/text match										

Emergent Reader Checklist

Teacher Directions: During whole-group, small-group, or independent reading time, observe children as they are engaged in the reading process.

Concept	Date of Entry			
Enjoys listening to books				
Confidently participates in shared reading				
Makes meaningful predictions using the story and pictures as clues				
Retells stories and rhymes				
Approximates book language Example: Child reads–*Me and my dog like to play.* Text reads–*My dog and I like to play.*				
Uses pictures to comprehend text				
Realizes that print carries a message				
Demonstrates book handling skills				
Locates the name of the author and illustrator				
Recognizes parts of a book (cover, title, title page)				
Demonstrates directionality: left-to-right				
Demonstrates directionality: top-to-bottom				
Identifies uppercase and lowercase letters				
Demonstrates an understanding of letters and words				
Identifies some sounds				
Matches spoken words to print				
Recognizes his/her own name and common environmental print				
Reads some one-syllable and high-frequency words				
Chooses to look at or read books from a variety of sources				
Can sit still for short periods of time to read a book				

Name:_____Date:_____

Early Reader Checklist

Teacher Directions: During whole-group, small-group, or independent reading time, observe children as they are engaged in the reading process.

Concept	Date of Entry			
Enjoys listening to books				
Confidently participates in shared reading				
Makes and confirms predictions using context clues				
Makes and confirms predictions using graphophonic clues				
Retells longer stories in correct sequence with some details				
Recalls facts from nonfiction texts				
Relies on word cues more than on picture cues to comprehend text				
Uses prior knowledge to help comprehend text				
Uses decoding skills to help comprehend text				
Self-monitors reading by asking: *Does that make sense? sound right? look right?*				
Notices miscues and attempts to correct them				
Rereads to check meaning				
Recognizes and reads an extended core of high-frequency words				
Reads in phrases or chunks				
Makes some text-to-self connections (Relates a part of the text-to-self)				
Makes some text-to-text connections (Relates one text to another text)				
Shares feelings about text with confidence				
Chooses to read independently				
Chooses to explore a variety of genre				

Name:_____ Date:_____

Comprehension Strategies Checklist

Teacher Directions: During whole-group, small-group, or independent reading time, observe children as they are engaged in the reading process.

Strategy	Date of Entries		
Using and Extending What You Know			
Activates existing background knowledge			
Builds background knowledge			
Determining Important Ideas and Themes			
Identifies main ideas or themes			
Compares and contrasts information			
Drawing Inferences			
Makes and confirms predictions			
Asking Questions			
Asks questions to clarify meaning			
Asks questions to understand key themes			
Synthesizing Information			
Connects ideas from text-to-text (relates one text to another text)			
Connects ideas from text-to-self (relates a part of text-to-self)			
Sequences ideas and story events			
Classifies and categorizes information			
Retells story events or key facts			
Creating and Using Images			
Creates and uses images from all senses			
Visualizes information from text, illustrations, diagrams, and so on			
Monitoring/Using Fix-Up Strategies			
Rereads text			
Uses decoding skills			
Self-monitors by asking questions: *Does it make sense? Does it sound right?*			

Using Anecdotal Records

Anecdotal records may be the easiest assessment tools to add to your assessment repertoire. Anecdotal records can be taken unobtrusively, and the time needed to take them is very minimal. You need no special training to assess children using anecdotal records, and they can be used on a daily basis. The following organizational systems will help you get started using anecdotal records today.

Anecdotal records can be taken for any subject. Be sure to date your anecdotal records and record the subject matter so you can quickly look through the records and find patterns within a particular subject. Once a month, spend five to ten minutes rereading the anecdotal records on each child. Look for patterns to tailor instruction in your classroom.

1/9–Reading: Juan located the word "see" in his guided reading book.

1/12–Center time: Juan was able to fluently form the word "see" with magnetic letters at the Word Zone center.

1/18–Writing: Juan spelled the word "see" in his journal as "se" in a sentence he wrote.

Evaluation: Continue to point out the word "see" to Juan in shared and guided reading sessions; encourage him to practice forming the word with magnetic letters and then write it on the chalkboard until fluent

Juan Alverez

Anecdotal Record Organization #1

Write each child's name at the bottom of a 4" x 6" ruled index card. Then, using a clipboard, lay the index cards onto the clipboard in a layered effect. Attach the cards, using tape.

As you plan your assessment opportunities, keep the clipboard and a pen with you. Then note behaviors you observe on his or her index card. Be sure to date your observations. Each day be sure to note behaviors for at least one-fifth of your class. That will allow you to have at least one anecdotal record for each child each week.

As you fill index cards, replace them and file the completed cards in your children's portfolios. During the fourth week of the month, evaluate anecdotal records, focusing on one-fifth of your class each day of that week. This will allow your evaluation time to be efficient.

Anecdotal Records Organization #2

Keep a supply of the anecdotal records grid on a clipboard. (See page 102) In each box, note a child's name. Each day be sure to note behaviors for at least one-fifth of your class. By the end of the week, your grid should be filled in with behaviors noted for each child in your classroom. Keep these completed grids in a three-ring binder for easy reference.

Each week you may decide ahead of time what subject to focus on or what skills to focus on. For example, at the beginning of kindergarten, you may decide to spend one week noting the kinds of books children choose to look at during their time in the Library Corner. When the week is over, reread your notes and begin to determine what kinds of books seem to interest a majority of the children in your classroom. If you find that many children choose nonfiction animal books, then be sure to share some nonfiction animal read alouds. Or perhaps, you want to branch their interests off in a new direction.

Anecdotal Records Grid

Teacher Directions: Label each box with a child's name. Make copies and keep them on a clipboard to record daily anecdotal records.

Tips for Taking Anecdotal Records

- **Keep your anecdotal record system close at hand.** This will allow you to note behaviors quickly.

- **Be sure to date your records.**

- **Set goals for the number of anecdotal records you will make each day.** For instance, every day of the week you may want to make notes on one-fifth of your children.

- **Choose a focus for your anecdotal records each day.** This may be particularly helpful if you are just beginning to use anecdotal records in your classroom. For example, the week of February 19th, you may want to note what kinds of writing each child is engaged in during Writer's Workshop.

- **Keep your anecdotal records positive.** Rather than noting what a child **can't** do, note what he or she **can** do instead. For example, *Today Mary was able to navigate a return sweep while reading her guided reading book.* Don't worry about the fact that she wasn't able to match the written words entirely with the spoken words. Focus on what children can do. This will help your instruction to remain positive.

- **Set aside time, at least once a month, to review and evaluate your anecdotal records.** Note any patterns you find amongst a group of students or a pattern you see emerging with one particular child.

- **Use your anecdotal records to guide your instruction.** For instance, if you have a group of children who are having difficulty with one-to-one correspondence when writing, you may want to pull them together in a small group and model this concept for them. If you note a group of children who are having difficulty retelling stories, pull them together in a group to work on retelling simple stories. These examples illustrate the use of anecdotal records to inform your instruction.

ABC Knowledge Assessment

Assess children's alphabet knowledge at the beginning of the kindergarten year (in the first month), mid-year, and at the end of the year. This assessment will help you tailor your letter recognition instruction.

Preparation for the Assessment

Copy the ABC Knowledge Assessment on page 106 on cardstock. Additional copies can be used as individual recording sheets for each child in your class.

Assessing Children

Work one-on-one with a child. Show the child the ABC Knowledge Assessment card. Say to the child:

- *What are these?* Do not use the word *letters* as you will want to note what the child's response is to these symbols.

- Reveal one row of letters at a time. Point to each letter and say, *Tell me what this is.* The child may respond with the name of the letter, the sound of the letter, or a word that begins with that letter. All are considered correct. Note each type of response given.

- Continue revealing one row of letters at a time as the child identifies each row.

Using the Assessment Results

As you look at the results of the ABC Knowledge Assessment, look for patterns among your children. For example, if a lot of children are having difficulty distinguishing between *b* and *d*, you can be sure to point out these letters in shared reading books and in the modeled writing you do. You can also create activities in the Word Zone that will give children the opportunity to sort and match *b*s and *d*s. Also, take time to work with children in small groups.

Group children by the letters they had difficulty recognizing or by the way they named the letters. For example, if a group of children had more difficulty recognizing lowercase letters than uppercase letters, group these children together and practice matching uppercase letters with their lowercase counterparts. For children who consistently named letters by the letter sounds, work on making connections between the letter sounds and the letter symbols.

As the year continues, be sure to compare each individual child to his or her earlier ABC Knowledge Assessments. This comparison can give you valuable information and help you to focus your lessons. In addition, it can be a great source of help for parents who aren't sure how to help their children at home.

ABC Knowledge Assessment

Child's Name: _____ Date:_____

Child's Age:_____ Child's Score:_____/54

Ask, *What are these?*

Child's response:_____

Point to each letter and say, *Tell me what this is.* Record responses in the following ways:

✓ = **correct response** (Note whether the child identifies the letter by its letter name (N), its letter sound (S), or by a word that begins with that letter (W).

x = **incorrect response**

o = **no response**

a___	e___	i___	m___	q___	u___	y___
b___	f___	j___	n___	r___	v___	z___
c___	g___	k___	o___	s___	w___	a___
d___	h___	l___	p___	t___	x___	g___
A___	E___	I___	M___	Q___	U___	Y___
B___	F___	J___	N___	R___	V___	Z___
C___	G___	K___	O___	S___	W___	
D___	H___	L___	P___	T___	X___	

Oral Reading Records

Oral reading records are assessments that are used to help determine a child's reading level, his or her strengths and weaknesses with reading strategies, and his or her comprehension of the text. They are meant to be quick assessments, something that you can do on the run. As you practice them, you will find that you don't need fancy forms to complete this type of assessment. All you will need is a sheet of paper, a pencil, and a calculator.

As you take oral reading records, many times you will take them on texts the child has read one time so he or she is familiar with the story. This type of oral reading record provides a great way to make sure that your guided reading groups are meeting the instructional needs of your children.

Other times you will take oral reading records as a more formal assessment of a child's reading progress. These texts are often unfamiliar to children. The purpose behind these kinds of oral reading records is to assess what a child does when he or she comes across challenges that he or she has not met before. When taking these kinds of oral reading records, you will want to give children a short introduction to the book and allow them a few minutes to look through it.

How to Take an Oral Reading Record

The best way to begin using oral reading records in your classroom is to jump in and try it. Don't worry if you miss recording some things the first few times around. Keep that in mind, however, when you score the assessments.

Sit down next to a child with a copy of the oral reading record form on page 112. The child should have control of the book to be read. Look over the child's shoulder to see the text that he or she is reading. If possible, do an oral reading record on one hundred words of text. This is not always possible with emergent texts.

Accurate reading: As the child begins reading the text, you will make checkmarks (✓) to illustrate accurate reading.

> **Example:** Child: ✓ ✓ ✓ ✓
> Text: I love to play.

Substitution: When the child makes a substitution to the actual text, write down the substitution instead of a checkmark. If time permits, write down the actual text underneath what the child read. Otherwise do this afterward. Substitutions are considered an error if the child does not self-correct.

> **Example:** Child: ✓ like ✓ ✓
> Text: I love to play.

Repetition: Whenever the child repeats a word, you need to record this by placing an **R** next to the checkmark. If the child repeats a phrase, draw an arrow to the beginning of the rereading. This behavior is not considered an error.

> **Example:** Child: ✓ ✓R ✓ ✓   **Example:** Child: ✓ ✓ ✓R ✓
> Text: I love to play.   Text: I love to play.

Omission: Whenever a child forgets to read a word, record this omission with a dash (–) instead of a checkmark. This is considered an error if the child does not self-correct.

Example: Child: ✓ ✓ – ✓
Text: I love to play.

Insertion: If the child inserts an extra word into the text, record this insertion with a caret. Write the word the child inserted above the caret. This is considered an error if the child does not self-correct.

                                       outside
Example: Child: ✓ ✓ ✓ ✓ ∧
Text: I love to play.

Self-correction: When the child realizes a mistake has been made and self-corrects independently, still record the error as it was made. However, place **SC** next to the error to show the child's ability to self-monitor. The original substitution no longer is considered an error. It is considered a self-correction. When you analyze the oral reading record, you will analyze it as both an error and a self-correction.

Example: Child: ✓ like **SC**   ✓   ✓
Text: I   love   to play.

Teacher Assistance: If a child gets stuck and does not appear to be able to continue with the reading, you may help the child in order to get him or her reading again. Mark the words that you told the child with a **T**. This is considered one error.

Example: Child: ✓ ✓ ✓
Text: I love to play. **T**

Analysis of an Oral Reading Record

Now that you know the basic symbols for taking an oral reading record, how do you analyze it? The first step is to record in the **E** (errors) column the number of errors made in each line of text. The next step is to record in the **SC** (self-corrections) column the number of self-corrections that were made in each line of text. Remember, self-corrections are not counted as errors, although you may want to analyze them as errors first and then again as self-corrections to help you determine why the child did what he or she did.

After recording the number of errors and self-corrections, use the formulas at the top of the oral reading record form to figure out the accuracy percentage and self-correction rate. These scores can give you an idea as to how your children are reading.

To really use this assessment tool as a way to guide your instruction, you need to analyze the errors and self-corrections made. That's where **M**, **S**, and **V** come into play in the **E** column and the **SC** column.

In the **E** column, ask yourself for each error made, *What cueing systems did the child use when he or she made that error?* For example, if the child read, *I like to play* instead of *I love to play*, then the child was using meaning (M), or the semantic cueing system. The sentence still was grammatically correct so he or she was using syntax or structure (S), also. What was lacking was the use of the visual (V) or graphophonic cueing system. Apparently, the child did not pay attention to the last three letters in the word *love*. So for this error, you would note in the **E** column **M** and **S**, but not **V**.

In the self-correction column, ask yourself for each self-correction made, *What cueing systems helped the child to make the self-correction?* For example, if the child read, *I like to play* instead of *I love to play*, but then reread and corrected his or her reading to *I love to play*, then the child probably went back to the visual or graphophonic cueing system to correct the error. You would then mark a **V** in the self-correction column.

Once you have finished this analysis, you will want to look for patterns that begin to emerge. Ask yourself some of the following questions to help look for these patterns.

- Did the child make one type of error over and over again? If so, what kind of error was it?

- Did the child attempt to problem-solve when encountering challenges? If so, how?

- Did the child ask for assistance when encountering challenges? If so, how often?

- Did the child self-correct many of the errors? Which kinds of errors were self-corrected? Which kinds of errors were not?

- Was this text at the correct reading level for the child?

- What kinds of errors did the child make in previous oral reading records? Has this pattern continued or improved?

- What do I need to do in the next guided reading session with this child that can help him or her to improve his or her reading?

Oral Reading Record Form

E=Error	SC=Self-correction	M=Meaning	S=Syntax	V=Visual

Title:_____

Student:_____Date:_____

Book Level:_____ Total Words:_____

Total E:_____ Total SC:_____

Accuracy Percentage:_____ Self-correction Rate:_____

95-100% accuracy = Independent

90-94% accuracy = Instructional

Below 90% accuracy = Frustration

Total Miscues + Total Self-corrections ÷ Total Self-corrections = Self-correction Rate

Total Words − Total Miscues ÷ Total Words = Accuracy Percentage

Page	Text	E	SC	E MSV	SC MSV

Tips for Taking Oral Reading Records

- **Try to sit right next to the child.** Body language is a great indicator of how the child responds to reading challenges. Notice whether the child looks to the picture for clues. Notice if the child uses his or her finger to reread silently or to read on silently. Notice if the child begins to mouth the word to himself or herself. These observations can be added as side notes to the oral reading records.

- **Try to not become reliant on pre-printed text when taking oral reading records.** Some reading programs provide oral reading records with preprinted text; however, if you always need to have the text preprinted on the oral reading record form, you will find you don't take oral reading records as often as you should. When you can sit down with a blank sheet of paper and record the child's reading, you will find that the ease of taking oral reading records is greatly improved. No preparation is needed. It is not necessary to have the full text in front of you when you look back at the oral reading records. The behaviors that you have noted and the analysis that you have done become the important pieces of the assessment, not the exact text.

- **Take time to analyze your oral reading records and compare them to prior oral reading records.** This is how you will notice emerging patterns. The analysis of the oral reading record is what helps you to formulate a plan for further instruction.

Retelling Form

Ask the child to tell you what the story was about. Do not prompt with any questions. Give the child time to tell you what he or she can about the story first. Then, if necessary, prompt the child to tell you more with questions like, *Where did the story take place? Who were the characters in the story? What happened at the beginning, middle, and end of this story?*

	Spontaneous Discussion	Prompted Discussion
Setting		
Characters		
Events		

Spontaneous Discussion

The child's comments were:

Relevant	5 4 3 2 1
Detailed	5 4 3 2 1
Enthusiastic	5 4 3 2 1

Overall Comprehension

Excellent		Adequate		Poor
5	4	3	2	1

A Balanced Literacy Writing Workshop

As you plan your daily schedule, attempt to plan at least an hour for your Writing Workshop time. The following writing components should be a part of the Writing Workshop:

- Modeled Writing

- Shared Writing

- Guided Writing

- Independent Writing

These components fall into the daily Writing Workshop schedule in the following way:

5-10 minutes: Warming Up Activities (Modeled Writing)

15-30 minutes: Whole-group Instruction (Shared Writing)

30-50 minutes: Small-group Instruction (Guided and Independent Writing)

10-15 minutes: Whole-group Instruction/Sharing Time (Modeled Writing and time for sharing what children have accomplished during their Independent Writing time.)

Modeled Writing

Modeled writing is just that–the modeling of writing done by a proficient writer. The writing is often done on the board or on chart paper where all children can easily see the writing. As you demonstrate the writing process, children see the physical act of writing, and they hear the thought process involved in writing as you share your thoughts aloud. You demonstrate how to decide on a topic, how conventions of print work, the challenges you must overcome, and so on. Just as in the read alouds, it is important to give children the opportunity to see and hear how proficient writers write.

Modeled writing is often a very daunting instructional strategy for teachers to implement in their balanced literacy Writing Workshop. They may feel unsure of their own writing skills; however, it is extremely important to spend five to eight minutes every day modeling writing for children. You are indeed a proficient writer. You write every single day–notes to parents, reminders to yourself, grocery lists, "to do" lists, and so on. You probably don't write a short story or a poem everyday, so when choosing what to write about and the type of writing to model, remember that you have lots of topics to choose from for each modeled writing session. Try writing about:

- what you had for breakfast

- the things you must do when the children leave to go home

- the list of groceries that you need to pick up in order to make dinner

- the thank-you note to your sister for your birthday gift

- a poem to include in a get-well card

- the class field trip you recently took

- a book review of a read aloud the class enjoyed recently

The modeled writing that you do for children should remain short and to the point. Think about your objective, share that objective with children, and do enough writing to get that objective across. At the beginning of the kindergarten year, your modeled writing sessions may focus on things like:

- how to put spaces between words

- how to navigate a return sweep

- how to use capital letters and periods

- how to write a simple sentence

- how to make a list of topics to write about

- how to write captions for pictures

As the year progresses, you will want to assess children's writing to look for challenges they are having difficulty overcoming. When you see a pattern in a group of children's writing, you may want to focus your modeled writing instruction on problem-solving that challenge. For example, if children seem to be having difficulty focusing on one topic, write a short story about one topic. Explain to children how your story only talked about your dog. It did not talk about your neighbor's dog or the family trip to the zoo. Let children's writing help to drive your modeled writing instruction.

Shared Writing

Shared writing is a collaborative effort between you and the children in your class. You act as the scribe while children help you to decide what the message of the writing should be. Language experience stories are a common shared writing experience. As you write down children's ideas, you will want to point out conventions of print such as, *I started the sentence with a capital letter.* You may also want to focus on spelling strategies, the writing process, and how to organize thoughts on paper. Shared writing should occur in the classroom several times a week. At the start of the year, you will want to keep your shared writing topics short so that they may be completed in one sitting. As the year progresses, you can start a story on one day and continue writing about that topic on another day. Here are some ideas to get you started.

Today at school we...

My friends and I...

When we went to the zoo (farm, apple orchard, and so on)...

When we looked out the window this morning, we saw...

We laughed so hard when...

On the playground, we like to...

We took a trip to...

Today we learned about...

Today we are going to...

The weather today...

Guided Writing

Guided writing is similar to guided reading in that children have more control of the writing task. Children are responsible for working their way through the writing task as you guide them. They may choose their own topics to write about. These topics may be related to something they have read in a guided or shared reading session, or topics may be related to something that has happened in the classroom. Children are expected to take ownership of the topics about which they choose to write. As they begin to put their thoughts down on paper, you can confer with children, prompting them for additional information about their topics, prompting them to remember the conventions of print, and prompting them to stretch their words out and listen for the phonemes.

Guided writing can take place in small groups similar to guided reading groups. It can also occur on an individual basis. As you work with small groups or individuals, decide on a focus for your instruction based on the needs of the children. Then guide them as they write based on that focus. For example, if the use of end punctuation is your focus, guide children on how and when to use end punctuation as they write. You are a guide while they control the paper, pencil, and message.

Independent Writing

The goal of all writing experiences in the classroom is to lead children to become independent writers, who are able to choose their own topics to write about, who understand print conventions, and who are able to reread and revise their own writing. As you work with children, encourage their independence and build their self-esteem by praising their writing strengths.

To encourage independent writing, you may want to brainstorm with children a list of topics they can write about. Keep this list posted in the classroom for children to reference.

As the year progresses and children have had more exposure to a variety of writing formats, encourage them to use those formats as they write independently.

Writing Assessments

The following writing assessments can be integrated into your balanced literacy classroom. Some of the assessments are informal such as a writing behaviors checklist, while others are more formal such as a writing dictation assessment. If these assessments are new to you, try to gradually fit them into your assessment repertoire.

Checklists:

Writing Behaviors Checklist
Emergent Writer Checklist
Early Writer Checklist

Other Assessment Tools:

Anecdotal Records
Writing Spree
Writing Dictation

Writing Behaviors Checklist

As you look at children's writing and talk to them about what they have written, note the behaviors that are evident in their writing.

Name															
Uses labels and captions															
Retells personal experiences															
Writes about personal experiences															
Has an awareness of beginning, middle, and end story structure															
Writes messages from left to right and from top to bottom															
Writes messages that make sense															
Uses letters in writing															
Phonetically spells words															
Correctly forms letters of the alphabet															
Uses spacing between letters and words															

Emergent Writer Checklist

Teacher Directions:
Observe children during whole-group writing experiences and independent writing experiences.

Name:_____

	Date of entries			
Makes pre-letter writing marks on paper				
Writes letters, symbols, or numerals randomly				
Writes some uppercase and lowercase letters of the alphabet				
Demonstrates directionality of letters				
Writes initial consonants				
Writes partially phonetically spelled words				
Writes some completely phonetically spelled words				
Writes high-frequency words randomly				
Writes a few known words correctly				
Uses random finger pointing when reading his or her writing				

Early Writer Checklist

Teacher Directions: Observe children during whole-group writing experiences and independent writing experiences. Most kindergarten children will not exhibit all of these writing behaviors, but many of them will exhibit some.

Name:_____

	Date of entries			
Writes uppercase and lowercase letters of the alphabet				
Writes messages that move from left to right and top-to-bottom				
Writes completely phonetically spelled words				
Begins to hear and use medial vowels				
Begins to hear and use ending sounds				
Writes an extended core of high-frequency words correctly				
Allows adequate spacing between letters, words, and sentences				
Uses basic capitalization rules				
Uses basic punctuation rules				
Demonstrates one-to-one correspondence of written to spoken words				
Uses a variety of prewriting strategies to plan writing (drawing, talking, webbing)				
Writes to communicate thoughts and ideas				
Chooses to write about a variety of topics				
Writes narratives based on personal experiences				
Demonstrates an understanding of story sequence (beginning, middle, end)				
Connects related ideas in writing				
Uses a variety of writing forms (realistic, fantasy, personal experience, humorous, and so on)				
Rereads writing to check for meaning				
Identifies some misspelled words in own writing				
Exhibits some knowledge of regular spelling patterns (CVC, CVCe)				
Chooses to write independently				

Writing Spree

To assess the words a child is able to write and to recognize in print, ask the child to write all the words he or she knows on a sheet of paper. Give the child a time limit of no more than ten minutes. At the beginning of the kindergarten year, you may want to start with a five-minute time period. Some children may only write a word or two at the beginning of the year. By year's end, they may be able to write six or more words.

At the start of this task, do not prompt the child to write any particular words. If you notice that child is not attempting to write anything, you may want to prompt with some of the following ideas. Make note of the ideas that you prompt as part of your analysis of the writing spree. When the time period is up, do not ask children to read their words to you. This is not an assessment of their reading ability but of their writing ability.

Prompts:

- Can you write your name? Can you write any family members or friends' names?

- Can you write *I* or *a*? Prompt with additional high-frequency words.

- Can you write any color words?

- Can you write the names of things you eat?

- Can you write words for things you do such as *run, jump*, and so on?

- Can you write animal words?

- Can you write words for things you do at school?

- Can you write words for things in your house such as *bed* or *table?*

- Can you write words for things you ride on or in such as *car* or *bike*?

- Can you write another word that is like the word *dog*? For example, *dogs.*

- Can you write a word that rhymes with another word you've written? (*cat, bat*)

Scoring the Writing Spree:

- One point is given for each correctly spelled word.

- One point is given if the word includes a reversed letter that does not represent a different letter. For example, if a child writes *bog* when prompted to write *dog*, then the child would not be given a point. If you did not prompt the child to write *dog*, and he or she wrote *bog* then assume the child spelled the word correctly and assign one point.

- One point is given for words written from right to left **if** the child actually wrote the words from right to left. If the child meant to write *me* and wrote *em*, writing the *e* first, no point is given.

- One point is given to each word in a word family. For example, if the child writes *read*, *reads*, and *reading*, three points are given.

- If the child uses an uppercase letter in the middle of the word while the rest of the letters are lowercase, the word is considered correctly spelled. One point is given.

NOTE: The scores of children may reflect the kind of reading and writing instruction taking place in the classroom. Children in programs that emphasize lots of writing or word learning may write many words within the time period. If instruction does not allow children to write often or standard spelling is not an emphasis, children may write a number of words but incorrectly.

For children who are not making progress in the number of words they are able to write with each new spree, help them attend to the intricacies of visual print. Although these children may be reading without any problem, they may not be making the connection between reading and writing. Engage them in lots of guided writing. Help them notice how the words they read look the same as the words they write.

Writing Dictation

To assess how well children are able to hear and write the sounds they hear in our language, ask them to write a sentence that you dictate to them. This assessment tool will help you to evaluate children's abilities to . . .

- connect letters to the sounds they represent. Children need to be able to connect both single letters and clusters of letters to the phonemes, or sounds, they represent.

- visually understand the symbols or letters children see and use in print.

- hear sounds that are embedded within words.

Several examples of dictation sentences are given on page 130. Each sentence has a total possible score of fifteen phonemes or sounds. Use a different dictation sentence each time you assess children. To give this assessment to children, ask them to listen carefully to the sentence that you read to them. Tell them you will repeat the sentence, reading it more slowly. Ask them to write the sentence down as you read it to them slowly.

Dictation Stories

Ask children to listen carefully to the sentence that you are going to read to them. Then tell them that you will repeat the sentence, reading it much more slowly. Tell them you want them to write the sentence down as you read it to them slowly.

Story #1:

Mom baked a cake today.

M o m   b a k e d   a   c a ke t o d ay.
1 2 3   4 5 6 7   8   9 10 11 12 13 14 15

Story #2:

My dad likes his bike.

My   d a d   l i ke   s   h i s   b i ke.
1 2   3 4 5   6 7 8   9   10 11 12   13 14 15

Story #3:

I like to play at school.

I   l i ke   t o   p l a y   a t   s ch oo l.
1   2 3 4   5 6   7 8 9   10 11   12 13 14 15

Scoring the Dictation:

- Each sound that is to be scored has a number under it.

- If a child adds letters to a word, these are ignored. Do not deduct from the child's score. For example, if the child wrote the word *read* as *reade*, the child would still earn three points, one point for each phoneme (/r/, /e/, /d/).

- If the child substitutes a letter that makes the same sound as the correct letter, the child receives credit for that phoneme. For example, if the child write *lice* for *like*, he or she would get all three points for that word. A substitution like *e* for *y* when *y* makes the long *e* sound would also be acceptable.

- If a child reverses letter order, the child loses one point for the word total. For example, if the child write *em* for *me*, he or she would only get one point for the two phonemes in that word. If the child wrote *readign* instead of *reading*, he or she would get five points instead of the full six points for that word.

Parent-Teacher Connections

© 2003 Rigby

As we all know, parents play a vital role in the education of their children. They are their children's first teachers. As we begin the school year, it is important to build a bridge between school and home right away. Without the support of parents, the teacher's job becomes much more difficult.

One way to get parents involved in their children's schooling is to encourage parent volunteers to be a part of your daily classroom activities. They are many ways to involve parents in the classroom. Here are just a few:

Set up a guest reader each week. Invite parents to come in the week before to choose a book to read aloud to the class. Then encourage them to practice reading it so they can model fluency and expression.

Invite parents to read with children in small groups or one-on-one. At the start of the year, focus parents' time on reading aloud to children. As the year progresses, some children may choose to read to parents instead. This small group or one-on-one attention is important for those children who have not had much experience at home with books.

Ask parents to act as scribes for children. During Writing Workshop time, particularly at the start of the year, parents can help those children who are hesitant to put any thoughts down on paper. Again, as the year progresses, parents can provide a listening ear as children read their stories aloud.

Invite parents to help you publish children's writing. They may type children's stories on the computer and bind them into books for the children to illustrate. These published stories can be written by individuals or compilations of class writing.

Encourage parents to join in a shared reading or guided reading session. As observers, they can learn a lot about how to discuss books with their children at home.

Invite parents to roam the room at literacy center time. Parents are great resources for student questions. They can also be helpful in keeping center supplies maintained. Parents can even join groups such as the Word Zone center to help organize activities with children.

By involving parents in the classroom, you are providing opportunities for them to learn from watching you interact with children. Leave curriculum instruction in your hands, while encouraging parents to lend a supportive hand as children work on becoming responsible learners and practice what they have learned.

Help parents understand what they can do at home to help their children with reading and writing. Two letters are included on the following pages that give parents effective tools for working with their children at home. It is vital for parents to involve their children in reading and writing activities at home.

Dear Parents:

Reading to your child is an important part of your child's reading development. Here are some things to keep in mind as you schedule time to read with your child.

✔ Make time to read to your child every day.

✔ Read a variety of texts: predictable books, rhyming books, fiction picture books, nonfiction picture books, the comics section, and so on.

✔ Reread your child's favorite books. Although you may become tired of reading the same story over and over again, children gain comprehension through hearing the same story repeated. Likewise, when children want to read the same story over and over again to you, allow them to do so. This repetition will help your child with his or her comprehension and reading fluency.

✔ Chant poems and rhymes and sing songs with your child. This engaging word play helps children to develop their understanding of how language works.

✔ Talk about the pictures in a book. This helps children expand their background knowledge, build vocabulary, and make predictions.

✔ Visit your local library. Be sure to check out story times at the library or local bookstores.

✔ Read with expression. Children need to hear how proficient readers become engaged in the books they read.

✔ Honor books by modeling how to care for them. If your child sees you taking care of books, he or she will begin to understand that books are to be valued.

✔ Give books as gifts. This helps your child to see that reading is special.

✔ Use book language, such as author, illustrator, front cover, pictures, captions, and so on. Often we take it for granted that children understand these terms when we use them; however, they may need clarification of these terms.

Sincerely,

Date:_____

Dear Parents,

Reading and writing go hand in hand as children develop a sense of what it means to be a literate person. You may be reading to your child on a daily basis, but don't forget to write daily as well. Here are some ways you can encourage your child to write at home.

✔ **Model writing** by inviting your child to watch and listen as you write the grocery list, the chores list, or the list of friends to be invited to a birthday party. As you create a list, read it aloud and talk about some of the characteristics of the words. For example, *We need to get butter at the store. Butter starts like bird ... b ... It starts with a b.*

✔ **Invite your child to help you write** the grocery list, the chores list, or the list of friends to be invited to a birthday party. Encourage your child to make connections with sounds and letters as he or she writes.

✔ **Provide your child with a variety of writing supplies** such as notebooks (don't worry that he or she doesn't use the lines to write on), blank paper, postcards, and so on. Provide markers, pens, pencils, and crayons for your child.

✔ **Encourage your child to help you write a personal letter** to Grandma or Aunt Kelly or Uncle Mike. Although you may need to do the actual writing, ask your child to provide you with ideas for the writing. Of course, ask your child to write his or her name at the end.

✔ **When your child shows you something that he or she has written, ask him or her to read it to you.** Do not worry if your child does not have a word written for every word said aloud. One-to-one correspondence comes with time and practice. If your child has forgotten what he or she wrote, encourage talk about an accompanying picture if possible.

✔ **Most of all, have fun with writing at home.** Point out all the different ways you write each and everyday–on the calendar, reminder notes to family members, grocery lists, notes to the teacher, and so on.

Sincerely,

Parent-Teacher Connections Through Home Activities

On the following pages, are some additional ways that parents can be involved with reading and writing activities at home. These activities can be copied and sent home with parents during the school year as you see fit, or they can be used to create a summer packet of reading and writing activities for reinforcement or enrichment.

The activities are based on concepts about print and emergent reading and writing behaviors. Encourage parents to spend at least ten minutes daily involved in reading and writing activities with their children. Not only will they gain new knowledge about their children's reading and writing strengths and weaknesses, but they will be sending a message that tells their children how important reading and writing are in our daily lives.

Purpose: To understand that pictures help readers to understand the text on a page.

1. Sit with your child next to you as you read a book together. The book may be a library book, one you have at home, or one you have borrowed from school.

2. As you read the book to your child, spend a minute talking about each picture in the book. Sometimes you will want to talk about the picture before reading the text on the page. This will help children to understand that pictures give them clues to what the text is going to say. At other times, you will want to talk about the picture after you read the text on the page. This will help children to understand that pictures support the text we read.

3. As your child reads books to you, be sure to remind him or her that pictures can lend a hand to better understanding the book.

Purpose: To understand text is read from left to right and from top to bottom.

1. Sit with your child next to you as you read a book together. Use a book that has a simple layout of text on each page. For example, all the text is at the bottom or all the text is at the top of the page.

2. As you read to your child, point out to him or her that you are starting to read from the left side of the page and moving to the right side. When you get to the end of a line, you can occasionally prompt your child to tell you where you should go next. This helps children to understand the idea that we read from left to right.

3. As you read, you will want to point out that you start reading text at the top of the page (or wherever the text begins, if there is writing only at the bottom part of the page) and that we move down to the bottom of the writing. Again, this will help your child understand how print works.

4. As you open a book, ask your child to point to the place where you should begin reading. As you turn each page in the book, make it your child's job to get you started reading in the correct place by having him or her point to where you should begin reading.

Purpose: To understand the concept of words and how they are separated by spaces on a page.

1. Sit with your child next to you as you read a book together. Use a book that has a very limited number of words on each page.

2. Read the first page aloud to your child, making sure that you point to each word on the page. Then ask him or her to point to each word with you as you reread the page. Show your child how to count the number of words on the page. You might say, *Look, there are five words on this page. One, two, three, four, five. There is a blank space in between each of the words. The blank spaces help us to know when one word ends and another word begins.*

3. Continue this routine for a few pages. Then finish reading the story without interruption.

4. After reading the story, have your child turn to his or her favorite page in the book. Ask your child to count the number of words. If your child needs help, have him or her follow along with you as you count the words.

5. Another way to help your child understand the concept of a word is to write a simple sentence on a piece of paper. Be sure to leave plenty of space between words. Then ask your child to circle each word in the sentence. Again, emphasize the space between words.

Purpose: To understand the concept that words are made up of letters.

1. Sit down with your child next to you at the table. Ask your child to tell you something about his or her day. Write a simple story about your child's day on a piece of paper. Be sure to print carefully, leaving noticeable space between words.

2. After you have written down your child's story, reread it aloud. Tell your child that his or her story is made up of words. Point to and read aloud a few of the words used in the story.

3. Then ask your child if he or she notices what each of the words is made up of (letters). You might say, *Look at all the letters I wrote. Each of the words (point to a word as an example) is made up of letters.*

4. Have your child point randomly to a word in his or her story. Read aloud that word and ask your child to identify the letters that make up that word. Repeat this several times, helping your child identify the letters if necessary.

5. Then ask your child to find several letters that you name. Each time he or she finds a letter that you name, read aloud the word that letter is in. For example, *Find a word that has the letter 't' in it. Yes, the word 'cat' has the letter 't' in it.*

6. As your child writes stories and shares them with you, emphasize the concept that words are made up of letters.

Purpose: To understand that words are made up of sounds.

1. Sit down at a table with your child and ask your child to repeat these simple words: *cat, ten, pin, box, sun.* Then say each of the words one at a time and slowly. After you say each word, ask your child questions such as *What sound do you hear at the beginning of the word? What sound do you hear in the middle of the word? What sound is the last sound you hear in the word?*

2. Remind your child that words are made up of sounds. As your child reads and writes, he or she needs to be able to hear the sounds in words. By saying the words slowly and stretching them out, children are more likely to hear the sounds in the words.

3. Another way to help your child understand that words are made up of sounds is to say a simple word aloud and slowly, stretch out the sounds for your child to hear. *Listen to this word. D-a-d. I hear three sounds in that word.* Then draw three lines on a piece of paper. Repeat the word slowly. Then talk about the beginning, middle, and ending sound in the word *dad.* As your child gets comfortable with this, you may want to challenge him or her with words that have more or less letters than the actual sounds they have. Be sure to point out when two letters say one sound. For example, the word *day* has two sounds, /d/ and /ā/.

Purpose: To understand that there are some words that need to be read and written quickly without sounding them out.

1. As we read to our children, we rarely have to stop and sound out a word. Most words have become automatic for us to read and write. Children also need to have a repertoire of words that they can read and write quickly without having to sound them out. Words such as *the, can, they, see,* and other high-frequency words are ones that we expect children to learn and be able to use without having to stop and labor over trying to sound them out.

2. The following words are the fifty most common words in print:

the	his	were
of	they	we
and	I	when
a	at	your
to	be	can
in	this	said
is	have	there
you	from	use
it	or	an
he	one	each
was	had	which
for	by	she
on	word	do
are	but	how
as	not	their
with	what	if

3. Spend time focusing on each of these words with your child. Ask him or her to look for the word in a book you are reading together. Or ask your child to write a sentence using that word. Encourage your child to write the word quickly, without stopping to sound it out. Make a game out of it and ask your child to write the word as many times as possible in one minute's time. This will help to make the word an automatic word for your child. Remember to keep it fun!

Purpose: To understand that writing carries a message.

1. Children often enjoy writing messages to moms and dads. When they give us the messages, we often see something that is not comprehensible to us. In order to encourage children to continue writing, it is important to praise them and ask them kindly to read their writing to us. This is the beginning of helping children to realize that their writing carries a message.

2. As your child moves from scribble writing to writing letters to writing words that actually resemble the words they are meant to be, it is always important to have your child read his or her writing to you. Praise your child for the accomplishments he or she has made. *Wow! Look here! You know the word dog starts with a **d** and ends with a **g**. That's great!*

3. Here's another way to help children understand that writing carries a message. Ask your child to tell you a short story. As he or she tells the story, write it down on a piece of paper. Then read the story back to your child. Be sure to point to each word so he or she can begin to understand that each spoken word has a written word connected to it. Then encourage your child to read the story aloud. Emphasize the idea that the story's message remains the same every time you read it.

Purpose: To understand that stories are retold in sequence.

1. This concept is one that can be worked into everyday life very easily. At the end of the day, you may talk with your child about the events that took place that day. Be sure to sequence your ideas by using the words *this morning, this afternoon, tonight.* Encourage your child to tell about his or her day in the correct order also.

2. After reading a story together, ask your child to tell you about what happened first, next, and last in the story. Use the words *first, next, last* or *beginning, middle, end.* This will help your child to understand the concept of sequencing.

3. After seeing a movie or a TV show, ask your child to tell you what happened first, next, and last. You might ask your child what his or her favorite part of the show was and when that happened.

4. You can extend these activities by writing sentences that tell what happened first, next, and last. Read these sentences aloud. Then mix them up and ask your child to put them in the correct order.

5. As sequence fits naturally into your everyday lives, encourage your child to retell events in the correct order.

Purpose: To understand the idea that some words rhyme.

1. Playing with language is important to children's literacy development. Being able to see the relationships between words helps readers to be able to solve challenges in their reading. For example, if I know what the word *cat* looks like, and I come to the word *flat* in the book I'm reading, I can use what I know about *cat* to help me read that word.

2. Expose your child to lots of rhyming patterns. Nursery rhymes are an excellent source of fun with language. Talk about which words rhyme and how you know they rhyme (they sound the same at the ends of the words). Encourage your child to fill in the blank at the end of a line in a familiar nursery rhyme.

3. Play rhyming riddle games with your child. *I'm thinking of a word that rhymes with* **see.** Then encourage your child to come up with a word that rhymes with your word.

4. In addition to saying nursery rhymes with your child, read nursery rhymes and point out the way the rhyming words look. Dr. Seuss books are great for pointing out rhyming words and patterns.

Purpose: To identify story elements such as character and setting.

1. Characters and settings of stories are basic story elements of which children should be aware. As children become aware of these elements in the stories they hear read aloud to them, they can then use that knowledge when they try their hands at writing their own stories.

2. As you read a story to your child, talk about the characters. Talk about whether they are real people or make-believe. Talk about whether they are funny characters or serious characters. Encourage your child to describe the characters. Use the word *characters* as you talk about this story element with your child.

3. Talk about the setting of the story–the time and place. Be sure to use the word *setting* as you talk about the time and place of the story.

4. When your child writes a story for you, ask him or her to identify the characters and the story's setting. If your child isn't able to do that, talk through the story and point out places where the setting could be added into the story or where the characters might become more realistic.

Purpose: To understand that readers can use what they already know or have experienced to help them understand what they are reading.

1. When we read, we often make connections to the text based on our own experiences in life. We draw on our background knowledge to make sense of topics that are not familiar. We make comparisons between characters in different books. We draw on our travels to be able to connect to the story's setting. This comes fairly naturally to us; however, we must help our children to make those connections.

2. Before reading a book, ask your child to predict what the book might be about by looking at the cover, reading the title, and paging through some of the illustrations inside. This helps your child immediately draw upon his or her background knowledge. For example, if the book is about the ocean, encourage your child to tell you what he or she knows about the ocean. This sets your child's mind up to use background knowledge and make connections with prior knowledge.

3. As your read with your child, encourage him or her to make connections with the characters by asking questions such as *How does this character remind you of yourself or someone else you know? How is this character like the character we read about in last night's story?*

4. Always encourage your child to connect what he or she reads to other books, experiences, or background knowledge. This helps us to make our reading more meaningful and enjoyable.

Appendices

Appendix A Word Family Cards

Copy these cards on cardstock. They can be used for activities in the Word Zone to help children become more familiar with common rimes (ending patterns). They have symbols to help children match up the correct pairs.

cat

bat

rat

hat

bed

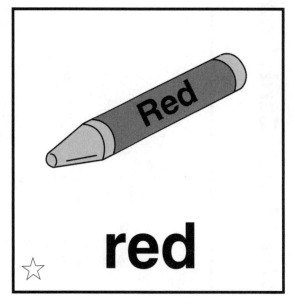

red

stick

chick

lick

sick

bug

tug

Word Family Cards (continued)

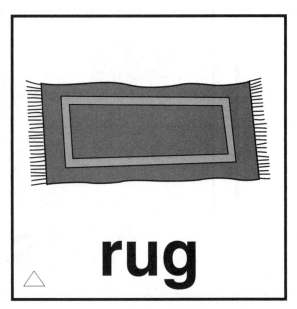

rug

hug

mop

hop

shop

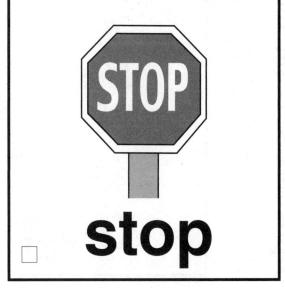

stop

Appendix B   Singular/Plural Cards

Copy these cards on cardstock. They can be used for activities in the Word Zone to help children become more familiar with singular and plural forms of words.

hat

hats

cat

cats

dog

dogs

tree

trees

pig

pigs

boat

boats

Singular/Plural Cards

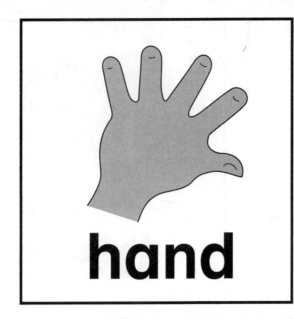

hand

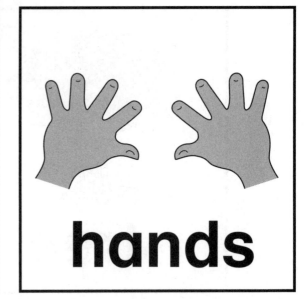

hands

bike

bikes

car

cars

Singular/Plural Cards (continued)

jar

jars

lid

lids

bed

beds

Appendix C High-Frequency Word Cards

Copy these cards on cardstock. They can be used for activities in the Word Zone to help children become more familiar with high-frequency words. They you see fit. The words listed are the top 25 most frequent words. They make up one-third of all printed material.

a	and
are	as
at	be

for	from
have	he
his	I

in	is
it	of
on	the

they

that

this

to

was

with

you	or
one	had
by	word

but	**not**
what	**were**
we	**when**

your	can
said	there
use	an

each	which
she	do
how	their

Appendix D　Beginning Sound Cards

Copy these cards on cardstock. They can be used for activities in the Word Zone to help children become more familiar with beginning sounds. They are helpful with both phonemic awareness and phonics instruction.

bike

bus

dog

doll

fish

fan

girl

goat

hat

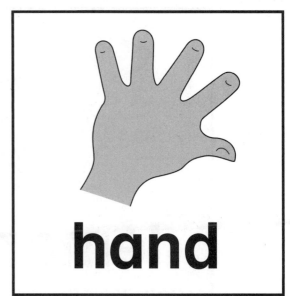

hand

jelly

juice

Beginning Sound Cards

kite

kitten

lemon

lion

mouse

moon

Beginning Sound Cards (continued)

nose

nuts

potato

pasta

ring

rose

sun

socks

turtle

ten

van

violin

Beginning Sound Cards (continued)

watch

whistle

yo-yo

yak

zebra

zipper

Appendix E Letter Cards (lowercase)

Teacher Directions: Copy these cards onto heavy cardstock and laminate for extra durability.

a	b	c
d	e	f
g	h	i
j	k	l
		m

n	o	p
q	r	s
t	u	v
w	x	y
z		

A B C

D E F

G H I

J K L

M

N O P

Q R S

T U V

W X Y

Z

References

Cambourne, Brian. *The Whole Story*. New York, NY: Ashton Scholastic, 1988.

Cunningham, Patricia M. *Phonics They Use*. New York, NY: HarperCollins College Publishers, 1995.

Fisher, Bobbi. *Joyful Learning*. Portsmouth, NH: Heinemann, 1991.

Fry, Edward Bernard, Jacqueline E. Kress, and Dona Lee Fountoukidis. *The Reading Teacher's Book of Lists*. Portsmouth, NH: Prentice Hall, 2000.

Holdaway, Don. *The Foundations of Literacy*. Portsmouth, NH: Heinemann, 1979.

Parkes, Brenda. *Read It Again!*. Portland, NE: Stenhouse Publishers, 2000.